OVERCOMING RELATIONSHIP PROBLEMS

2nd Edition

A self-help guide using cognitive behavioural techniques

OVERCOMING

MICHAEL CROWE and KEVAN WYLIE

ROBINSON

ROBINSON

First published in Great Britain in 2017 by Robinson

Copyright © Michael Crowe and Kevan Wylie, 2017

Previous edition *Overcoming Relationship Problems* written by
Michael Crowe and published by Robinson, an imprint of
Constable & Robinson Ltd., 2005, 2010

1 3 5 7 9 10 8 6 4 2

A CIP catalogue record for this book is available from the British Library.

Important Note
This book is not intended as a substitute for medical advice or treatment.
Any person with a condition requiring medical attention should consult a
qualified medical practitioner or suitable therapist.

ISBN: 978-1-47213-874-3

Typeset in Bembo by Initial Typesetting Services, Edinburgh
Printed and bound in Great Britain by Clays Ltd, St Ives plc

Papers used by Robinson are from well-managed forests and
other responsible sources

Robinson
An imprint of
Little, Brown Book Group
Carmelite House
50 Victoria Embankment
London EC4Y 0DZ

An Hachette UK Company
www.hachette.co.uk
www.littlebrown.co.uk

Contents

Acknowledgements
(First Edition, 2005)

I would like to acknowledge my debt to the late Robin Skynner, whose teaching and example were an inspiration to many couple and family therapists, including myself.

I would like to thank Jane Ridley for permission to quote some of her clinical case material in this book. I would also like to thank her and my other colleagues and students at the Maudsley Hospital Couple Therapy Clinics for their enthusiasm and creativity. I would like to express my gratitude to Jack Nathan and Jill Thompson for their careful and helpful reading of the manuscript.

Finally I would like to thank my wife Diane, who has not only put up with me for thirty-seven years, but has also given me much encouragement in the task of writing this book.

Note

The 'cases' we have reported in this book are based on couples seen in therapy, but names and recognisable details have always been changed.

Michael Crowe

Foreword
(Second Edition)

It is now twelve years since the first edition was published, and it was felt that the book, which has had a wide circulation thanks to the Reading Well library project, needed to be brought up to date. This would have been difficult with MC as the sole author, since he is now retired from clinical work. It is fortunate therefore that KW, who worked in the same clinic, uses similar treatment methods, and is more in touch with developments in sexual medicine, was able to join the project. We hope that our combined efforts will make a useful and relevant contribution to the field.

Michael Crowe

Kevan Wylie

PART ONE

RELATIONSHIPS AND RELATIONSHIP PROBLEMS

1

About relationships

Introduction

Why do we need a book like this?

Most adults spend the major part of their life in an intimate relationship. The fact that you are reading this book probably means that you are either in a relationship or would like to be in one. Relationships are potentially very satisfying, they save us from loneliness and protect our physical and mental health. A two-parent family is also the most successful setting for the care and upbringing of children. But there are many problems that can cause disturbances in these relationships. These are not just arguments, power struggles and fights, but may also include stress reactions, depression or anxiety in one or both partners. Problems such as jealousy and sexual difficulties can often cloud what might otherwise be a successful relationship.

The Couple Therapy Clinic at the Maudsley Hospital, in which we were both involved, devised a form of therapy for helping these problems. It is chiefly on this experience in treating couples that this book is based.

Do-it-yourself couple therapy?

You may wonder whether this type of book can be used by couples on a 'do-it-yourself' basis. Well, much of our therapy in the clinics at the Maudsley was directed towards giving our couples 'homework' exercises to be carried out before our next meeting with them. The couples themselves were therefore responsible for quite a lot of their own successes in therapy, and many of the exercises we devised are included in the various sections of the book. So we think it is very likely that our recommendations will be helpful.

How will this book help?

Our aim is to help you to learn new ways of dealing with the kind of problems that crop up every day, problems which if repeated day after day may undermine the foundations of the relationship and can lead to breakup. The focus is on the practical side, and wherever problems are mentioned we have tried to suggest a possible solution.

How should you read the book?

At the first reading, you will probably be sitting quietly on your own. But this means that, if you have a partner, only half of the relationship is getting the information, and it would be good to share the ideas with your partner as soon as you are able to do so.

Sometimes of course the person reading the book will have a partner who doesn't want to get involved in discussing the relationship. You could still read it yourself, making use of the suggestions in Chapter 5 for those working unilaterally to improve their relationship, and things might get better as a result.

You can of course select which part of the book to start with, and we have included a number of cross-references from one chapter to another, so that you can follow your interest through different chapters.

The Three Sections of the Book

- The first section (Chapters 1 to 3) is about relationships and the problems that can arise in them. There is a chapter on sexual relations in this section because we think it is important not to leave sex out when discussing relationships generally, as if it was part of a separate world.
- The second section (Chapters 4, 5 and 6) is about how to improve your communicating and negotiating skills, and how to balance the various pressures on the relationship from family members, children and work.
- The third section (Chapters 7 to 12) covers special areas such as dealing with sexual problems, illnesses, psychological problems, violence, divorce, 'blended' families (families with stepchildren), and lastly how to get into a relationship if you don't currently have a partner.

Couple relationships today

Couple relationships today are in a state of flux, with a high divorce rate and an increase in single-parent families, blended families and families with same-sex parents, and it is not at all clear how the situation will change over time. Couple relationships, however, will probably endure as a way of living because they provide stability and comfort for those who are involved in them, and they are the best way we know of providing a secure setting for raising children.

The wide variety of heterosexual relationships

The variety of these relationships today is much wider than would have been thought acceptable fifty years ago. Today we see married couples, couples bringing up children without being married, and also couples who have a steady sexual relationship but choose not to live together. There are also many people who get married but then change their partners through divorce (sometimes described as serial monogamy). As a result of divorce, and also because many women have decided to have children without living with the father, many children now live in one-parent households. Blended families, where there is a step-parent sharing the care of the partner's children, are also very common (see Chapter 11).

Same-sex relationships

Gay and lesbian relationships are now respected in a way that would have been impossible in the past. They are no longer illegal in Europe or in the USA, although they remain so in around seventy countries of the world. Since December 2005, civil partnerships are also now legal in most European countries and American states, and most of these now also recognise same-sex marriage. It is increasingly common for same-sex couples to bring up children. We should say here that, although most of the case examples in the book are of heterosexual couples, they should be relevant to same-sex couples as well, in that the problems encountered by them are basically very similar to those encountered by heterosexual couples, and should be amenable to similar solutions.

Relationship problems are often similar whatever kind of relationship you are in

These problems are much the same, whether we are looking at short-term or long-term, heterosexual or same-sex relationships, and whether we are considering European, African, American, Arabic, Asian or Australasian cultures. It is these common problems, occurring in most kinds of relationship, which we will be dealing with throughout the book, and for many of them we will try to offer possible solutions.

The pressures on couple relationships

The likelihood of divorce

The pressures on marital and long-term cohabiting relationships have greatly increased in recent times. In the UK, the number of couples getting married, including second marriages, decreased year on year between 1996 and 2011, although there was a slight increase in 2012. In the same period the number of divorces increased (39 per cent of marriages ended in divorce in 1996 and 42 per cent in 2012)[1]. Divorce is for many a relief from the tensions that they have experienced in the marriage, and there is some evidence that, both for the couple and for their children, a good divorce can be better than a bad marriage. However, divorce may bring its own problems and stresses (see Chapter 10).

Traditional and modern views of marriage

In the nineteenth century, marriage was seen as a means to respectability, women were expected to submit themselves to the will of their husbands, men were expected to provide for the family, and children were expected to be 'seen and not heard'. Divorce was difficult to obtain, and couples often stayed together in spite of their mutual antagonism. With the rise of individualism, and also feminism, in the twentieth century, many changes have occurred in the status and stability of marriage. With increasing life-expectancy a marriage now could potentially last much longer than it would have done in the nineteenth century. In the West, the continuation of a marriage depends on an ongoing agreement by both partners to keep it going, and too much 'taking each other for granted' may lead to a loss

---

1   Office of National Statistics, 2014

of this agreement and therefore to separation or divorce. In more traditional (mainly Asian) cultures, however, there is a strong sense that divorce is a stigma, and is to be avoided.

Equality within relationships

The concept of the 'modern man' has been around for the last fifty years or so. This involves the man in sharing household chores, looking after children, and even in some families being the house husband, or main carer for children. It is a very good ideal to aim for, and in some couples it works satisfactorily. It is, however, the woman who tends to take responsibility for household matters in many 'modern' relationships. In same-sex relationships, the partners may seem more equal than heterosexual couples, but actually these couples also often settle down to a kind of traditional division of labour, with one of the two being more conscientious over household matters while the other deals more with the outside world. In one way, however, same-sex partners have an advantage over heterosexual partners, in that the common male–female misunderstandings (see Chapter 3) are avoided.

Starting a relationship (see Chapter 12)

Meeting a partner

Whatever the specific cultural or social pressures on a couple, there is a sequence of events which is fairly uniform and which almost every long-term relationship goes through sooner or later. The first part of this process is meeting and becoming attracted. In Western societies this often takes the form of 'falling in love', although this is by no means the only way of starting a relationship, and in some ways carries a greater risk of instability than moving from friendship to dating, or even having a traditional 'arranged' marriage.

Happily ever after?

If the couple do fall in love, there is usually a stage when they idealise the relationship and each other. Some authorities have likened this to a form of temporary insanity in which the person in love loses contact with reality, and may even suffer from ideas of being all-powerful, or believe that everything will be perfect for them forever. 'They lived happily ever after' is the typical ending to a fairy tale, and some lovers believe this about themselves.

When the differences emerge

This situation does not usually last very long, as other realities make their presence felt. The clash of personalities may often be the first problem encountered, for example one partner wanting to spend money freely while the other wants to save. They may disagree about politics or religion, they may have friends who don't get along with their new partner, or they may have different educational backgrounds, or different sexual drive levels. All these will conspire to weaken the heady feeling of being in love. On the other hand, this loss of an idealistic honeymoon situation could be seen as giving the partners the opportunity of getting to know each other as real people, becoming more realistic and 'growing up' in the process.

The need for tolerance and understanding

There is a real need for interpersonal skills to understand and resolve these differences between partners. Tolerance, understanding, negotiating skills and the ability to solve conflicts are all-important (see Chapters 4 and 5). So is the ability to remain part of a couple rather than thinking of oneself as an individual who 'happens to be in a relationship'. In many couples the sexual side is strong enough to overcome these difficulties, and makes it worth the partners' while to make the relationship work. But in others these early stumbling blocks are fatal to the relationship and the partners separate.

Factors that favour stability

What then are the factors that help a couple to get together and stay together beyond the first few meetings? It is almost a cliché to say that mutual interests, combined with sexual attraction, help a couple to cement a relationship and maintain it. Here is a list of some of the factors found in research work to favour stability and satisfaction in a relationship.

The Foundations of a Good Relationship

- Mutual attraction
- Good clear communication
- Emotional understanding
- Negotiation and compromise
- Clear boundaries
- Commitment
- Both partners comfortable with intimacy (sexual and otherwise)
- Both partners comfortable with any power differences

Similar or different?

There are some people who value peace over excitement, while others would be bored without some drama in their lives. Sometimes two exciting people attract each other, and the same may happen with two quieter people.

The other side of the coin is the 'union of opposites', which many find to be more exciting and can be satisfying, as long as each partner doesn't expect the other to be a clone of themselves, and as long as they can tolerate the major differences that they usually encounter in each other.

Childhood influences

Another factor in the choosing of a partner is the influence of one's experience of family life as a child. There is often a subtle similarity between the partner one chooses and the parent of the opposite sex. This may take the form of a physical likeness, or it may be in terms of personality or ways of interacting. The psychoanalytic view of 'marital fit' (see Chapter 2) is that there is a kind of unconscious blueprint in everybody of the sort of partner they would like to have, based often on their experiences with parents. They choose a partner on the basis of factors they are unaware of and cannot easily understand.

The early stages

There is almost always a period of experimentation before the relationship becomes permanent. This is very variable in its duration, and may involve many false starts. The couple may meet in various ways, from being work colleagues to meeting at parties or on holiday, or increasingly nowadays meeting through the internet and various smartphone apps. They will often have to negotiate various issues: if and when to begin a sexual relationship, whether to declare their relationship to friends and/or family, and whether to live together.

These transitions will always be difficult, and will raise dilemmas about whether they are really now a couple or two individuals who happen to be close friends (see Chapter 12 for a more detailed discussion).

Transition stages

At different stages in the process, there are rituals which tend to be followed. For example, the decision to move in together, the engagement (and exchange of promises and/or rings), the arrangements for the wedding ceremony and so forth all have to be negotiated. This can be a crisis for the couple, and some couples have so much difficulty with this transition period that they split up as a result. Sometimes it has to do with the negotiations as to who is in charge: one partner may have very different expectations from the other about their life patterns in the phase following the engagement.

CASE EXAMPLE

Roger (28) and Caroline (29), who had had a good relationship before their engagement, moved in together, and then began to experience differences over their desire to socialise. Roger was a quiet person who preferred to stay at home in the evenings and sit by the television. Caroline had had a lively social life with friends, and became rather bored staying in. In therapy they worked out a compromise in which they would spend every Friday evening at home together, while Sundays were to be their socialising day, when they would either go out with friends or entertain at home. This enabled Caroline to get the social life she wanted while Roger was able to have the intimate 'couple' sessions that he valued.

Decisions at the time of moving in together

There are a number of issues that couples need to work out at the time they begin living together. These can range from the very practical, such as who pays the rent and other living costs, to more complex ones, such as how much of the couple's personal life to share with the parents of each partner. Similar problems arise when couples get married and have to make decisions about joint bank accounts or mortgages. The assumptions may be that they will carry on as their respective parents have done, but there may be serious differences of opinion about it, which they don't even realise exist until the crisis occurs. It is much better to sort these things out in detailed discussions before the couple marry.

The family life-cycle

Each family goes through several stages in its development. These are sometimes known as the family life-cycle. The idea, as it was first developed, is based on the typical nuclear family of the mid-twentieth century. Of course, not every couple or family goes through each stage, but it is a simple way of documenting the stage which a couple has reached, and can help to understand some of the stresses they are experiencing.

Stages in the Family Life-cycle

1. The couple meet and form a relationship
2. The couple get engaged
3. The couple get married
4. They have their first child
5. The first child goes to school
6. The youngest child leaves school
7. The youngest child leaves home (empty nest)
8. Retirement of one or both partners
9. Death of one partner

This is of course a very limited and rather stylised account of the progress of relationships, and in many cases the end stage is divorce rather than death. It takes no account of same-sex relationships, and the question of childless marriages, second marriages and non-marital cohabitation is not considered. However, it remains a useful way of thinking about family relationships, and may help the readers of this book to understand some of the particular stresses which they encounter at the points of transition. Dealing with changes in the family is something we will be covering in more detail in Chapter 6.

The influence of the family of origin

Many of the difficulties in relationships come from the

expectations that the partners come with, and these often derive from their experiences in their families of origin.

Openness within the family

One typical example of this which is quite commonly seen, is where one partner's family is outgoing and open while the other's is quiet and diplomatic. A case will illustrate the problems that might arise from this.

CASE EXAMPLE

Arnold and Angela had been married for three years, and they complained of misunderstandings which resulted in Arnold becoming withdrawn, while Angela felt angry and expressed her frustrations because he would not discuss the problems. Her family of origin had been one in which the members were always outspoken, often in conflict with each other, but they usually made up any differences as soon as the problems had been aired. His parents, in contrast, never had any arguments, and felt that conflict was a very dangerous thing which might lead to divorce. In therapy, the couple worked out a system of time-limited arguments (see Chapter 6), in which they could air their differences and then bring the discussion to a close by hugging each other and reassuring the partner of their love. This helped Angela to have the open discussions that she needed, while Arnold was not overwhelmed by the anxiety they caused because they were time-limited.

In this couple, the problems were partly caused by an inability to have 'good' arguments, and we will be covering the use of arguments as a way of helping your relationship in Chapter 6.

Household tasks

Another area of conflict based on the families of origin is that of the division of labour in household tasks. Many boys, even in today's atmosphere of equality, have not been in the habit of helping with domestic chores. As mentioned above, women are in most households more conscientious than men, and they end up doing more of the day-to-day work in the house. The influence of the families of origin may play a part in this problem too.

How to discipline children

One of the most common areas of conflict related to family of origin is the disciplining of children. Each partner feels that they know the right way to do this, based either on their own experience as children, or on trying to do the opposite to what their own parents did. Once again the parents of both partners will often be tempted to intervene and take sides with their own son or daughter. It may take a fair amount of discussion and understanding for the couple to work through these problems, and they should eventually reach a consensus which they can jointly agree on, and which does not rely completely on wisdom handed down from their families of origin.

Cultural differences

In this multicultural society, we see more intermarriage and more inter-cultural relationships than ever before. We are in a broadly secular society, in which there is growing toleration of difference, but in some couples the issues of culture can be a great source of stress. We cannot say that we know or understand all the differences between different cultures. It is important to emphasise here that no culture is seen as being right or wrong, superior or inferior. However, a description of some of the differences between cultures that may be observed in clinical work can begin to explain the stresses experienced.

The South Asian pattern

In South Asian cultures, whether Hindu, Muslim or Sikh, there are several fairly constant features. Marriage is traditionally considered the responsibility of the family and society rather than the individual. The wife, in more traditional families, is expected to go and live with the husband and his parents, and to be subservient to his mother (as in the case of Ahmet and Aisha).

CASE EXAMPLE

Ahmet (28) and Aisha (21), a Muslim couple had been married for two years, and had no children. They were both born in England but their parents came from Pakistan. They were complaining of not being able to have a satisfactory sex life, mainly because they lived with Ahmet's parents, and the parents insisted that they should sit up with them until late at night. By the time the couple eventually got to bed it was already time for everyone to sleep. In their culture, the wife has to go to the bathroom to wash after sex, and if they had intercourse Aisha was embarrassed about the parents knowing what they had been doing. There was, however, some pressure from both sets of parents for them to conceive a child, and so they were looking for help as a couple.

In therapy they were able to devise a plan to resist the pressure from the parents to sit up with them, on the excuse that they needed some time to themselves so as to get enough sleep to be fresh for their work the next morning. They were then able to have sex earlier, and so the bathroom problem was not so acute. This is an example of a cultural issue which needed to be overcome before a couple could have a normal intimate life together. It is also an example of setting boundaries around the couple which exclude other people, but are acceptable within their cultural limits.

There are other differences seen in Asian families. Divorce is frowned upon, and is indeed less common in this cultural group. These rules are of course not observed by all South Asian families, and here the more Westernised families act in much the same way as European families.

The African-Caribbean tradition

The African-Caribbean tradition is rather different, with a family centred around the mother, while the father may not necessarily be resident with the mother and the children. The mother is often referred to as his 'baby mother' rather than his partner or wife. He will usually contribute to the finances of the family, but will leave the upbringing of the children mainly to the mother. Again, this is the extreme situation, and many African-Caribbean families these days conform to the European pattern.

African families

African families tend to be quite traditional and male-dominated, like the South Asian families, but without the expectation for the wife to live in the extended family. However, in many African families the parents may entrust the upbringing of their children to relatives, even leaving them with relatives at home in Africa while the couple travel to the West for further education or training, or for career advancement.

Couples from different backgrounds

It is clear from the differences outlined above that there is a great potential for conflict in couples where they come from two different traditions. The assumptions that each partner makes about what is a good relationship, or what is the right way to live and bring up children, can be very different if they are from different cultures, and only by discussing the issues openly can they hope to come to an agreement. For a therapist working with couples and families, it is some-times difficult to find a good compromise. It is important to respect the differences between them and to give both of them a good hearing. The main aim is the stability and satisfaction of the relationship, and who is right or wrong is much less important.

Financial and social pressures

Financial pressures

Most couples experience financial difficulties, whether short or long term. As mentioned above, there may be a clash of ideals, with one partner wishing to 'live now, pay later', while the other prefers to live always within their means without borrowing money. Conflict often emerges over the decision on how to pay for accommodation, or whether to spend on an expensive holiday. However, spending on gambling, drinking or compulsive shopping can raise more serious issues. Usually the couple manage to compromise on financial issues, but in some the dispute is severe enough to threaten the relationship. There is no 'right' way to handle money, and each couple will make their own arrangements. Some individuals feel that it is helpful to keep some savings in their own name, however close they are with their partner. This may not imply an intention to separate, and it may actually make separation less likely because this person feels more secure on account of the savings.

Expectations fostered by the media

Pressures on the stability of relationships are also felt as a result of media publicity. There is at present a tendency to idealise marriage as an institution and at the same time to attack it. The media are full of stories about the marriages, infidelities and separations of celebrities. There are also regular features on how to improve your relationship and how to achieve a better sex life. This carries the risk that couples who take the media too seriously will look at their own relationship and conclude that, because it doesn't come up to standard, it is no good and they should separate. It hardly needs saying that you need to weigh these media pronouncements against your own experience, and not disparage the good things that you have in your own 'good enough' relationship.

How children affect the relationship

There are further pressures on those who have children, and many couples choose to delay having their first child until later in their relationship. The average age of first-time mothers and fathers continues to rise, and in 2014 was 30.2 and 33.1 years respectively. To have children is for some couples the main reason for getting together, and most couples would say that having children is a source of great satisfaction. However, the evidence is that couples with children are on average less happy in life than couples who are childless, although the satisfaction of bringing up children can certainly compensate for this. Children often test the parents in ways that they did not envisage, for example in misbehaving, in causing the parents to discipline and control them, in school refusal, in drug taking or in developing psychiatric illnesses or antisocial behaviour. We will come back to this topic later in the book, in Chapters 4, 6 and 11.

Sustaining a long-term relationship

This is a big topic, and the discussion of it will take up quite a high proportion of the rest of the book. At this point we are presenting a few of the factors conducive to a long-term relationship. It is important, however, to stress that there can be good relationships in which none of these things are present, and whatever your own situation, it is worth trying to improve things by putting the ideas in this book into practice.

Factors Which Can Help to Sustain a Long-term
Relationship (see also Chapter 12)

- Being realistic from the beginning and working on problems
- Developing mutual interests
- Toleration
- Shared ideals
- Ability to negotiate and compromise

- Sexual attraction
- Both partners comfortable with the level of intimacy that they have

On the other hand, there are also some factors which are more likely than others to break up relationships, and again we will simply list these at this point.

What Factors Might Lead to Separation?

- Affairs, especially if they lead to a new long-term relationship
- The resentment caused by an affair
- Drinking, drug taking, gambling, etc.
- Difficult or irresponsible behaviour
- Negative influence of friends or family members
- Pressures from work, travel, etc.
- Getting hooked on the internet (including porn sites)
- Conflict
- 'Growing apart'
- Retirement and the 'empty nest' (after children have left)

Any of the above factors may lead to a serious crisis in the relationship, but it is also possible to recover from almost any of them if the couple value their relationship enough, and sometimes working through the difficulties can strengthen a relationship and make it more stable and more satisfying.

The end of a relationship, whether due to death, separation or divorce

The process of grieving

Every relationship must have an end, one way or another. In today's society the majority of marriages still last until the death of one partner. The response to this loss may be very different for different individuals. In most bereaved partners, however, there is a period of 'shock and protest', which may be accompanied by a sort of denial that the person is really dead. There is then in most people a period of emotional outpouring and yearning for the partner, in which the dead person is idealised and any past conflicts or differences ignored. Over the course of time, there is usually a process of putting things into perspective; the bereaved person takes a more balanced view of the partner, and 'reattachment' takes place. This may be reattachment to other family members, to friends, to a new partner or to outside activities.

Eventually the bereaved partner comes to terms with their loss, and gets on with daily life. The whole process may last for months or years, and it often takes its toll on the health of the person who has been bereaved. Recent widows have poorer health than married women, and tend to go to their doctor more for minor complaints. They also have a higher rate of psychiatric illness, mainly depression. Widowers are more likely to neglect themselves in the year after bereavement, to drink excessive amounts of alcohol, to have more road accidents and to suffer more from heart disease and cancer. Again, these are problems which decrease over the years following the bereavement.

Prolonged or very severe grief reactions

Time usually heals those who are bereaved, although at times such as birthdays, wedding anniversaries and the anniversaries of the death, the feelings of loss and yearning are often increased. Sometimes, however, the mourning process goes on for a very long time, perhaps many years, and it may become a full-blown depressive illness, needing psychiatric treatment. In other cases, the grief takes on different forms, such as a complete immersion in work or other creative activities.

Some bereaved partners become involved very quickly in a new relationship 'on the rebound'. This may have a positive effect, although there is also a risk that the new relationship could be unstable because of the speed of its development and the fact that the bereaved person is not really at that time emotionally ready to make far-reaching life decisions. Other people after bereavement are determined never to replace the dead partner and decide to live solitary lives. There is no right or wrong way to behave in this situation, but it helps to be aware of the pitfalls which may exist for those who make hasty decisions.

Separation or divorce

An increasing number of relationships now end in separation or divorce (see Chapter 10). This may be a relief for one or both partners, and generally people who have been divorced are unlikely to go back to the same partner. However, the breakup of a relationship is never simple. Many individuals who have been divorced, especially if it was through the partner's initiative rather than theirs, experience the equivalent of a bereavement, and they may go through all the stages of mourning outlined above. After a separation it is harder to idealise the partner than it would have been if they had died, and the person who has been left may feel both extreme anger and jealousy towards them, especially if the partner is in a new relationship. In many ways, a divorce can be harder to bear than a bereavement by death, because there is less of the continuity of affection and love than would be felt towards a dead partner.

Care of children after a separation

Following separation or divorce, there is also the problem of the continuing care of the children of the relationship, and the difficulty experienced by two people who couldn't live together as a couple trying to cooperate on the delicate and vital task of bringing up vulnerable children. It is then that some of the skills outlined in Chapter 11 will be useful, including the role of the step-parent living with children whom he or she has taken on in a new relationship, and the problems of managing the interfaces between the ex-partner, the children and the new partner.

The health of divorced people

Divorced people, like those who are recently bereaved, have poorer health than those who are still married. Again this is most noticeable in the first few months after the divorce, but it remains so for a year or so afterwards. This underlines the advantages of working at a marriage or partnership while it is still viable, and hopefully this book will help couples to be tolerant and attentive, and thereby have a successful long-term relationship.

Key Points

- Couple relationships can be very supportive and satisfying for the partners, but problems arise for almost every couple at some stage of their relationship.
- There is a wide variety of types of relationship, but the problems they have are often very similar.
- Most relationships today are held together by voluntary agreement rather than by culture or the law.
- Problems may arise when the couple need to make adjustments in order to enter the next stage in the family life-cycle.

- Financial and social pressures can play a big part in destabilising a relationship.
- The influences of cultural background and of the partners' families of origin are usually quite strong.
- There are factors which lead to stability in a relationship and factors which lead to the risk of separation (see the Tables).
- There is always a need for toleration and negotiation.
- Couples should be realistic about their expectations, especially after the early stages of a relationship.
- Divorce can have a negative influence on health and well-being, but sometimes provides relief from intolerable stress.

2

Understanding relationships: the theories

Introduction

The three main theoretical bases for couple therapy are behavioural/cognitive, systemic and psychodynamic. These theories of human interaction are all trying to understand and manage the same phenomena, but they are radically different from each other. They may seem on the surface to be incompatible, but this is less of a problem if you realise that they are starting from different places.

Behaviour therapists look at individuals from the outside, and concentrate their attention on behaviour which can be observed and counted. Their work on operant conditioning with dogs, rats, pigeons and other animals has produced remarkable results, and has taught us a great deal about the psychology of motivation and repetitive behaviour, both in animals and humans. Behavioural methods have also proved effective in helping parents to reduce disruptive behaviour in their young children.

From a basis of behavioural understanding, but taking

a more 'interior' view of the individual, cognitive behavioural therapy was developed. This looks at the way that negative thinking can interfere with our self-esteem and our problem-solving, and helps us to substitute positive thought patterns to facilitate change (see below).

Systems theorists also look at human interaction from the outside, but are more interested in the ongoing patterns of behaviour in couples and families. They observe human relationships and conceive of them as a series of 'dances', with family members learning the steps and repeating the dances, which may often serve to keep the family together. Therapeutic interventions can alter the sequences so as to reduce problems that otherwise could disrupt family relationships.

Psychoanalysts, and others who work psychodynamically, see life and relationships very differently. Based on the pioneering work of Freud, they see unconscious impulses as the central spring of human activities, and see problem behaviour as the result of these impulses. They use introspection (looking inside the mind) and interpretation as ways of understanding the pressures and conflicts that we all suffer. Couple therapy can be carried out using psychodynamic theories, but we will not be recommending this type of therapy here, as it is not suitable for a 'do-it-yourself' setting.

Are these three theoretical views incompatible?

It may be argued that these three theoretical approaches are incompatible. Our belief, however, is that it is possible to use the three different theories to do different things. The diagram in Figure 2.1 shows how the three approaches all intervene at different levels of a couple's interaction, and might therefore be seen as being compatible with each other.

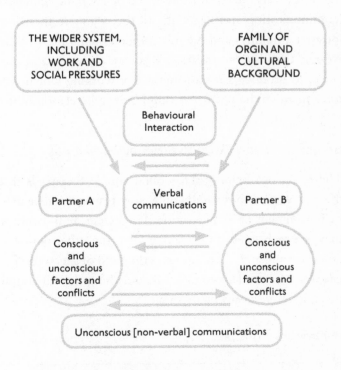

Figure 2.1 Behavioural, systemic and psychoanalytic interactions as they affect the couple

Putting the theories to work for relationship therapy

We have found in clinical experience that the best combination of approaches is what the team at the Maudsley have called the Behavioural-Systems Approach. This makes use of the very practical ideas of the behavioural therapists (communication and negotiation), the cognitive therapists (positive thinking) and the more wide-ranging ideas of the systems theorists (boundaries, alliances, closeness and distance) to produce a robust method of working which will solve many of the problems found in couple relationships.

Behavioural and Cognitive-Behavioural ideas

The basic idea behind behavioural couple therapy is that the best way to motivate people is by **reward**, rather than by punishment or by persuasion. If a couple are in conflict, they are each likely to be saying what the other person is doing wrong, and often this takes the form of a lecture. *'I've talked to him and talked to him'* is something that all couple therapists have heard many times.

Behavioural Principles

- An action that is rewarded is likely to be repeated
- An action that is ignored (extinguished) is less likely to be repeated

---

> - An action that is punished is interrupted: how-
>   ever, since punishment involves attention, the
>   punishment may be unintentionally rewarding,
>   and thus it is unpredictable whether the action
>   will be repeated or not

Behavioural couple therapists state that you should motivate each other, not by lecturing, but by doing the things the partner wants in return for the partner doing the things that you want (mutual reward). The principle is that a positive gesture can lead to a positive gesture in return, and that a more fruitful relationship can result from the change.

A second consequence from this is that if you don't like something that the partner is doing, the best way to change it is not to complain, but to ignore the behaviour (extinction) and to try to encourage an alternative positive action. Complaining and punishing the 'bad' behaviour doesn't help to reduce it, because punishment involves giving attention, which may be unintentionally rewarding,

These simple ideas may seem over-optimistic, but they have been proved time and time again in research to be a very effective way of helping couples. We will be following this up in Chapters 4, 5 and 6, when we deal with how to solve problems.

A second behavioural idea for improving a relationship is positive communication. The behavioural approach tries to encourage the two partners to mention it whenever something happens which they enjoy, and not to harp on the things they disapprove of. Again, there will be further examples of good positive communication in Chapters 4, 5 and 6, when we deal with how to solve problems.

The third aspect of behavioural couple therapy is based on cognitive therapy as developed by Aaron Beck. He has extended behavioural ideas to the inner workings of the mind. So, for example, he points to the tendency of people who are stuck with a problem to use 'negative thinking', which means that they assume that there is no solution. They also tend to generalise, believing that there is no answer to any of their problems, and not just the one they are dealing with. In couple therapy, Beck emphasised the need for each partner to examine his/her own ideas and to see if they could alter these negative thinking patterns, changing them to more positive ones, and beginning to work positively on the relationship.

Cognitive Behavioural Principles

- Negative patterns of thought keep depressive thinking going
- Positive self-statements can be used to counter negative thoughts
- This can reduce depression and pessimistic thought patterns

Systemic theories

These were developed in the context of work with families. They involve a wider understanding of relationships. One systemic idea is that around each person is a kind of invisible **boundary,** and the person will normally take measures to defend that boundary if someone steps across it. Each person has a private side that would be uncomfortable for others to enter.

Systemic Concepts

- Boundaries between people, including the generation boundary
- Hierarchies (treating children according to their age)
- The decider subsystem (the two parents deciding for the children)
- Circular causation (an endless chain of cause and effect)
- Homeostasis (keeping the status quo, because change is risky)

Other areas of systemic thinking relate to the boundary which exists around the couple who form an alliance together in relation to the outside world. So, for example, a wife may be discussing many of the intimate details of the couple's sex life with her mother, without the husband knowing, and this may be seen by him, when he discovers it, as a boundary violation, a kind of betrayal of him and their relationship.

Systemic theorists are also interested in hierarchies, which deal with the question of dominance and submission between individuals. For example, a mother may need to be in control of her five-year-old child to a greater degree than she is of her fifteen-year-old. She is not, however, necessarily in control of her husband's day-to-day behaviour. This leads to the concept of the 'generational boundary', whereby the parents form a 'decider subsystem' or alliance, equal with each other but jointly making decisions for the children.

Another important idea in systemic theory is the idea that families unconsciously try most of the time to keep things as they were. Thus some parents refuse to accept that their children are growing up and that they might deserve greater freedom than before. This is sometimes called 'homeostasis', a word that derives from the ability of the body to keep its temperature constant in spite of fluctuations in the outside temperature.

Probably the most important idea in systems theory is 'circular causation'. This is the idea that, when two people are in a relationship, they engage in a series of actions towards each other which are quite repetitive and which don't start from one person's initiative but can be seen as a continuous chain. The only way that one person could be said to be 'causing' a problem is if the chain of interactions is artificially 'punctuated'. Punctuation means starting your account of the incident from a particular action by Partner

A, so that A seems to be responsible for what happened: it would be just as valid to start your account from an action by Partner B, which would make B responsible. So it is not a question of who is to blame for the situation, but of trying to untangle the sequences of interaction which lead to the problem repeating itself.

CASE EXAMPLE

A simple example might illustrate the idea. A man comes in tired from work, and doesn't say hello to his partner. She becomes angry because of this and shouts at him. He tries to pacify her by giving her a hug, which she rejects. He goes out to the bar. Both of them blame each other for the tension that follows the incident, because each has ignored their own contribution to the problem and sees only the partner's unreasonable behaviour. If they had punctuated the scenario differently, they might have realised that they themselves had made a contribution, and begun to change the pattern.

Psychoanalytic theories

Although we will not be using psychoanalytic ideas in our 'do-it yourself' methods, they deserve some discussion because they can sometimes help to understand otherwise incomprehensible conflicts. For example, when people have insecurities about themselves they may treat their partner in a cruel or offhand way. These insecurities may have originated in earlier relationships, perhaps with parents. Sometimes when relationship problems drag on without resolution, you might think of getting a referral to a psychodynamic couple therapist who will tease out deeper conflicts that may be perpetuating the problem.

Psychoanalytic Concepts

- Bringing the unconscious into consciousness
- Unconscious conflicts affecting the relationship
- Defence mechanisms, including splitting and projection (e.g. putting all your own 'bad' motivations and feelings into your partner)
- Understanding the 'marital fit' (what the partners have brought into the relationship from their past)

Communication – verbal and non-verbal

Everyone communicates non-verbally, even if they are strangers in the same room. Think then how much more communication goes on between you and your partner. Non-verbal communication can be in the form of eye contact, smiles or frowns, tone of voice, posture, touch and the distance between you. The non-verbal communication between partners is a good indicator of the health of the relationship.

Research has shown that couples with a good relationship make regular eye contact, while those whose relationship is troubled rarely look at each other.

Many of the everyday contacts between partners are made non-verbally. A touch on the shoulder or a smile can indicate positive feelings, and reassure the partner that they are cared for, although they can also be misinterpreted if there is tension between you. Frowns can of course have the opposite effect. The tone of voice is a further indication of how you are treating each other.

Another aspect of the non-verbal communication is how close the partners are to each other when they speak. The nearer they are, on the whole, the less they need to raise their voices, and the more their communication will be peaceful and positive.

Their verbal communication is equally important, and may involve both positive and negative aspects. There is a tendency to make assumptions about the other partner, which may result in a misinterpretation that the partner is hostile or angry, when they do not actually feel angry. The partners then begin to cast blame on each other. A good general rule about communication is never to assume you know better than the speaker what he or she means! If in doubt, ask for clarification.

Good verbal communication is something which we all fall short of at times, but which is the basis of human interaction – without it we would live in a very confusing world. There are a few simple rules which couples should follow in communicating, which we will now outline.

Rules of Good Verbal Communication

- **Be brief and simple.** It is better to say less in a sentence than more, and then you should leave a gap so that your partner can reply to the point that is being made.
- **Leave frequent gaps.** This gives your partner a chance to respond. Monologues don't contribute to good relations. Good communication usually includes the possibility of reply.
- **Be positive.** There is a world of difference between the statement *'You are always undermining me'* (negative and critical) and the alternative statement *'I would like you to back me up even if you don't always agree'* (a request for help).
- **Always end with a positive, even if you have said something negative.** This avoids what we call the 'sting in the tail', where someone has said something positive and then follows it up with something critical. The trick is to change the sting-in-tail comment to one that ends positively. Thus *'You are making an effort now, but you have been difficult for a long time'* (sting-in-tail) could become *'I have felt for a long time that you were being difficult but I see you are now making an effort'*.
- **Be specific.** This means trying not to generalise too much, and keeping the discussion as

clear as possible. So there is a great deal of difference between *'You are always putting me down in front of others'* and *'I was upset when you criticised my driving when your mother was in the car'*. The second version at least makes it possible for the partner to address the issue and try to be less outspoken when a similar situation arises.

- **Suggest ways to act differently in the future rather than complaining about the past.** A proposed alternative is always more acceptable than a complaint. The hearer can always accept the suggestion, which can then avoid a stalemate or an argument.

- **If you can't avoid discussion of the past, ration it so that your partner knows that it won't last very long.** This could be done by planning a discussion time and setting a timer so that you both know when time will be up (see Chapter 5).

- **Stick to the topic and don't drift off into other areas.** The temptation is often to expand the discussion into other areas of disagreement. If there is no more that can be usefully said on the subject, the couple should stop talking about it and either change the subject or just go into separate rooms until things quieten down.

- **If you are talking *about* your partner, try not to 'mind-read'.** It is much better to ask your partner what they think about something than to tell them what you think they are thinking. If you are wrong in your guess this will just irritate your partner.

- **Try to start everything you say with 'I' rather than 'you'.** This is not always easy, and we will give some more specific advice in Chapter 5. The key thing to remember at this stage is that if you start with 'I', your partner can't claim that you are talking nonsense or that you have no right to speak for him/her.

Negotiation (see also Chapter 5)

This is quite similar to communication, but it takes the process forward one more step. If you want to change something which has been causing problems, you should try to put it in a way that your partner can make use of. A simple complaint may be sufficient to solve the problem, but as often as not a complaint leads to a defensive reply or to a counter-complaint. It is much more productive to put the complaint in a positive way, in the form of a request.

For example, if a woman wants her partner to stop leaving his socks on the bedroom floor, it would be better for her to ask him to put them in the laundry bag or in the washing machine (a positive request). If possible, this could be followed by an offer to do something in return, which might be in response to a request by her partner.

Requests should be positive, specific, future-orientated, repeatable and practicable. These will be dealt with in more detail in Chapter 5, but at this stage it may help to give an example of the kinds of requests which work and those which are ineffective. An impracticable request would be to ask the partner to stop drinking, because the request is negative. A better option would be to request a reduction in drinking, or to ask for a different pattern, for example to drink only on particular days of the week.

This type of interaction, termed reciprocity negotiation, is the one which has had the most research done on it over the past thirty years or so, and it has consistently come out as being a highly effective part of couple therapy and quite simple to carry out (see Chapter 5).

Systemic ideas: boundaries

In our lives we have to decide all the time where to draw the line in terms of boundaries. How close do you allow a new friend to get? How much of your personal life do you share with them? How much do you let them see if you are upset or depressed? Do you invite them home? Do you lend them money?

These boundary issues are very relevant in a new relationship. But the same questions apply to the boundaries in a long-standing relationship. How much do you disclose to your partner about your debts? Do you tell them if you find someone else attractive? Do you let them know about the fact that you have a serious illness?

Boundaries not only exist between partners, but also between the couple and the outside world. The couple has to work out a comfortable arrangement for what things are treated as confidential and what may be discussed with others. These questions will be taken up in Chapter 6.

Closeness, distance, dominance and submissiveness

Closeness and intimacy

Closeness and distance can be thought of as an example of the way in which people keep the boundary between themselves. A couple may be close in several different ways – sexually, in sharing ideas and plans, in emotional sharing and in non-sexual physical ways.

- Sexual intimacy will be looked at in detail in the next chapter, so we will not deal with it further here.
- The sharing of plans and ideas is something called operational intimacy. This means acting as a team, so that one member of a partnership knows more or less where the other one is at all times. Most couples will telephone each

other or use email to keep in contact. In some couples, however, there is very little operational intimacy, and they live separate lives except for the times they are together (e.g. at weekends or on holiday).

- Emotional intimacy has to do with sharing feelings, and by and large this is something that women do more readily than men. The popular book by John Gray suggests that the two genders are from different planets, which he terms Mars and Venus (see Chapter 3). In a heterosexual couple, there are often conflicts as to the amount of emotional intimacy they have, and one partner (often the woman) may express some resentment because she wants more emotional sharing in the relationship.

- Physical intimacy refers to touching each other in non-sexual ways. A well-known sign of an intimate relationship (for instance if a couple have not declared that they are an 'item') is if one partner picks a bit of fluff off the other's clothing. The lack of physical intimacy can be an ominous sign if a relationship is shaky.

Being close does not necessarily mean having weak boundaries, and it is possible to be close in any of the four ways mentioned above while keeping one's boundaries intact. It is more a question of having a clear understanding of the limits of personal space. So a couple who are close in an operational and emotional way, may make it clear that their professional lives are their own, and will be kept apart from the relationship.

The four types of closeness do not necessarily go together. It is quite possible to be close sexually but not to share emotions, and sometimes this causes problems for couples when one partner wants more emotional closeness while the other only wants to be closer sexually.

Dominance and submissiveness

A further complication in discussing this aspect of relationships is the question of which partner is dominant. Obviously in some relationships the dominance shifts according to the setting: the wife may take the lead where childcare is concerned, while the husband may lead over financial matters. However, there are many areas in which dominance is disputed. For example, a couple might have repetitive arguments about who has the right to make decisions, and these arguments may threaten the continuity of the relationship.

There are some couples in whom the dominance appears to be in one direction, but in fact, it is the opposite. This may be associated with 'illness behaviour' on the part of one partner. The 'ill' partner may appear to be much weaker than the other one, but the 'well' partner actually spends much time and effort in trying, almost in the role of a servant, to please the 'ill' partner and make him/her feel better. In other couples, the situation may be less overtly connected with illness, but simply reflect the ability of the apparently 'weaker' partner to control the 'stronger' one (see Chapter 8).

Most couples reach a state of equilibrium on the question of dominance, and they both take the dominant role where it is necessary, while at other times being quite democratic about who takes the lead.

The parental couple and hierarchies

When a couple have young children, it is usual for them to make decisions about the children without consulting them. This results in a hierarchical pattern of relationships in which the parents become the 'decider subsystem' and discuss things to do with the children's welfare without involving them in the process.

As the children grow up, the parents and children have to adjust to a new situation in which the children have to make some decisions for themselves. This can be difficult when the children and parents disagree on the degree of freedom and responsibility that the children should have. Teenage conflicts may arise, and in many families this is a healthy way to resolve the uncertainty. In other families, there can be a difference of opinion between the two parents about the management of the teenager(s), with the children beginning to take sides and often succeeding in their efforts to divide the parents. This is almost always bad for both the children and the parents, and leads to the teenager(s) having a sense of power associated with insecurity. It may also be associated with psychological problems and/or substance abuse in the teenager. This emphasises the need for the parents to act as a united team or 'alliance' in relation to their children.

There may be further difficulties in the family if there are children of different ages, and the parents are caught between their wish to give the older children more responsibility while at the same time treating all the children fairly. There is no perfect solution to this situation, and each family will have to work out the best compromise for themselves.

Repetitive sequences

Couples often find themselves repeating the same discussion or argument, and reaching the same unsatisfactory endpoint. The discussion might be one of 'symmetrical' responses in which one partner says something hostile and the other responds with a hostile comment (see Chapter 4).

Another type of repetitive interaction is where one partner complains repeatedly of a negative feeling (perhaps depression or anxiety) and the other tries to help. We sometimes call this a 'complementary' interaction, and the couple seem to be acting like nurse and patient or like parent and child. Once again it is difficult to get out of the habit of interacting in this way once it has become a regular feature of the relationship. We should emphasise that there is nothing either good or bad about symmetry or complementarity as such. All our interactions have some symmetry and some complementarity in them, but the problem in the examples given is that they are repetitive and stereotyped, leading to problems that are hard to get out of (see Chapter 6).

Symbols and anniversaries

The symbols of a relationship may be quite varied. Generally they are more central to women than to men. The wearing of a wedding ring is one example, and it is noticeable that married women almost always wear one, while it seems to be an option for married men. Another symbol of the relationship is the giving of cards and presents at birthdays, Christmas, etc. If this is forgotten, it can send a very bleak message to the partner.

Perhaps the most important symbol, however, is the wedding anniversary. In couples who are not married, there is often another date which is remembered, for example the first time the couple went out together, the first time they had sex, or the first holiday together.

As the family grows in size and in numbers there are more dates to remember, to do with the children and grandchildren. There are also many different ways in which the couple can cooperate – over children's activities, family events and matters to do with house maintenance. In all these areas there is a symbolic as well as a practical significance.

More minor 'core symbols' of the relationship involve regular habits that the partners may have got into, such as bringing a cup of coffee in the morning, eating together or sharing the bed. When there is a severe problem, some couples may feel that these rituals are unimportant and stop 'performing' them, and this can be ominous for the relationship.

When there are minor difficulties in a relationship, the maintaining of the core symbols can have a healing effect, for example when one partner after an argument brings the other one a drink or goes over and hugs them. This kind of simple intervention can make an enormous difference to an otherwise difficult partnership, and perhaps prevent a breakup.

Key Points

- The theories underpinning couple therapy are behavioural, cognitive, systemic and psychoanalytic.
- They are not incompatible, but apply to different levels of the relationship.
- The main behavioural principles involve rewarding positive behaviour and ignoring unwanted behaviour.
- The main cognitive principles are to think positively and avoid generalisation.
- The main systemic ideas involve boundaries, hierarchies and circular causation.
- The main psychoanalytic ideas relate to the unconscious and its influence in relationships.
- The methods used in the rest of the book are based on the behavioural-systems approach.

- Communication can be non-verbal and verbal.
- There are ten principles of good verbal communication (see pages 42–44).
- Reciprocity negotiation is a key technique in solving problems.
- Other issues discussed in the chapter include boundaries, closeness, dominance, hierarchies, alliances and repetitive sequences.

3

Sex, gender and the couple

Men and women: the similarities and differences

The differences between men and women have been well recognised since the earliest times. However, there has been a recent tendency, perhaps deriving from feminism and perhaps from the great publicity that sexual matters have had in recent years, for people to assume that women and men are not only equal but actually the same. It's true that many jobs are equally well done by both, and that some of the reasons that men have been better paid and promoted in their employment are to do with men's natural competitiveness, combined with an inbuilt historical unfairness in society. However, the differences between the genders are very clear and well known, and these have made it difficult at times for men and women to understand and appreciate each other.

Differences in brain function

There are some general brain differences between men and women, but these differences have only recently been understood in more detail. This is partly in the way that each gender uses the right and left halves as well as the front and back of each side of the brain. The left half of the brain handles logical thinking and verbal skills whereas the right side of the brain handles intuition and spatial ability. Women are generally more 'left brain' competent, and manage better in tasks that involve language and communication. Men are generally more 'right brain' competent, and therefore manage better in tasks that require spatial coordination, such as maths, physics and engineering. It has also been found that men have more connections from the front to the back of the brain facilitating connectivity between perception and coordinated action.

Women tend to have more connections between right and left sides of the brain facilitating communication between analytical and intuitive processing of information. In fact, whether from nature or from nurture and social pressures, most boys aged three will talk to other boys of the same age about cars, guns or computer games; girls of the same age will prefer to talk about their families and friends. Men are generally good with machines, many sports and practical things generally, while women are generally better at understanding people, chatting on the telephone, keeping in touch with lots of people and maintaining relationships. Although there are overall differences in the brains of men and women, for the vast majority of people there is a combination of masculine and feminine features. For this reason, it's probably more important for us to accept that men and women do not have that many differences inside their brains but that people all have a unique mix of this combination, making us all different from each other. Much of this will be influenced by how a child is brought up with repeated messages from inside the family and this can be influenced by cultural and religious messages.

Differences in psychological strengths

In a similar vein, girls and women are good at 'multitasking', and can keep many goals in mind at the same time without neglecting any of them. Boys and men, on the other hand, will concentrate on the job at hand, and leave other tasks to another time or delegate them to someone else. In this connection, women are usually better at looking after children, and manage to keep a focus on the kids in their charge while at the same time getting on with making meals and doing housework. Men can do all these things, but tend to forget one while concentrating on the other. They tend to want to get the children safely settled so that they can get on with other things. Increasingly, however, there has been an acceptance that there are not universal or specific gender profiles. So, whilst there may be certain differences in preferences and behaviour observed between men and women, this cannot all be attributed to distinct differences in the brain.

Cooperation and competition

Men are likely to be more competitive than women, and when you see two men or boys together they will often be making comparisons between the speed of their cars, the amount they earn, their achievements in sport, how new or powerful their smartphone may be or the size of their houses. This is perhaps related to the way in which in an animal setting males tend to compete for both status and the right to mate with the females in the herd. It is a natural pattern of behaviour, and is probably driven by testosterone. Women and girls, on the other hand, will form cooperative networks and put their ideas together without insisting on taking credit for a particular initiative. Again, in the animal setting, the females in the herd will often collaborate in bringing up the young, especially if the 'assistant carers' are related to the mother of the offspring.

How these differences affect relationships

These differences come to our attention when there is a relationship between a man and a woman. Early in a relationship, when sexual attraction is high and both partners are idealising each other and giving each other the benefit of the doubt, there is usually no problem. However, when the relationship is older and the couple are trying to solve difficulties that they encounter in the course of the average day, the differences between the male and female way of doing things comes to the fore. Men tend to be focused, logical and independent in their problem solving, whereas women tend to rely more on emotional cues and like to network in their approach to problems. How often do we hear the complaint from the man that 'we have discussed all this before, so there's no need to go over it again', as if the problem has been completely resolved, while the woman says, 'I know, but I still don't feel right about it.' There is no easy answer to this dilemma, and many couples have to deal with it by agreeing to differ or by going along with the more dominant partner's ideas. The bottom line is that for women the most important issues are often to understand the problem and each other, to be heard and to be taken seriously, while for the man it is more urgent to solve the problem and learn from doing so how to solve similar problems in the future.

The 'Mars and Venus' problems

John Gray, in his entertaining but also quite serious book *Men are from Mars, Women are from Venus*, makes an important point about the differences between men and women with respect to their relationship difficulties. Not only do they speak 'different languages' but they respond differently to the crises in their relationships. Men, he says, retire to their caves, withdraw and think out the problems and then come back with a solution (or without a solution). Women like to talk it over, and can't understand when their male partners don't seem to want to do this. Misunderstandings arise between men and women when they fail to realise that the partner doesn't react as they themselves would react.

The man may feel that he has done all that is necessary to be appreciated, and can't understand why the woman is being illogical in this way. The woman may feel that her partner is failing to understand that she has times (perhaps hormonally determined) when everything seems wrong, and that all she needs is to be given time and sympathy.

Sexual drive, sexual desire

Biological forces in men

The desire to be involved in sexual activity is a strong one throughout the animal kingdom. In most species it is the male who initiates sexual activity, and this happens largely through the influence of testosterone. Juvenile males in animal herds whose testosterone is low may have a curiosity about sex, but usually do not try to mate with the females, and the same is true of males who have been castrated and thus lost their main source of testosterone. What is true of male animals applies more or less equally to human males, in that in younger boys there is a strong interest in things sexual, which doesn't usually result in sexual approaches as such. However, there is in most mature human males a biologically driven sexual urge (or libido), as testosterone levels increase during puberty and are usually highest in the late teenage years and early twenties. There is a very gradual decline in testosterone levels starting when men are in their thirties and this drop is much steeper once men reach their eighties. It has been shown that testosterone levels drop faster in men who have diseases typically seen with aging and these include being obese, depressed or having cardio-vascular disease.

Biological forces in women

In females sexual drive is much more variable. In many animal species, the female is unresponsive to sexual activity most of the time, but highly responsive at the time of oestrus, when the ovaries produce their eggs and the female is fertile. In humans this does not happen, and the mature human female is potentially responsive most of the time. However, this responsiveness varies with the circumstances, for example being more active if she is in a rewarding relationship. In addition there is the hormonal cycle in women, which happens on a monthly basis throughout the reproductive years, except in pregnancy and the time just after childbirth. In many women there is a time of increased interest in sex on a monthly basis, but this varies: in some it is just after the end of the menstrual period, in others just before menstruation, and in others there is no preferred time for sex.

If changes in sexual desire are considered secondary to relational (or other) factors at a certain stage in life for the woman, the question of whether or not these should be considered problematic is discussed further in Chapter 7. A woman moving home, changing jobs and helping her children to attend a new school is likely to be exhausted but may react quite differently to another woman in similar circumstances. If the woman feels that her partner is supportive her response to a sexual advance is likely to be much more favourable than that from another woman where any involvement from the partner is construed as unhelpful. There is then also the menopause, a rather sharp cut-off point for the menstrual cycle, which is associated with a reduction in natural vaginal secretions. However, there is no uniform change in sexuality at this time, and many post-menopausal women are as interested in sex as before.

How gender affects sexual interaction

The sex hormone testosterone (an androgen) is converted into another sex hormone, estrogen, and this happens much more in women than men although we all have a combination of both hormones. These act by stimulating androgen and estrogen receptors in the brain and around the body. Emerging evidence is that it is the androgen receptors in both men and women that play an important role in sexual libido. All this means that men and women can have rather different hormonal influences on their libido, as men's testosterone levels are on average much higher. It is not only hormonal factors that are important, because attitudes towards sexual activity are also different. For men there is often a regular hormonal-led message that tells them that it's time they had another sexual experience. For most women, however, their sexual interest is much greater when they are in a satisfying relationship, and if there is no partner, women can go for a long time without wanting a sexual experience.

This is not universally true, but it seems to apply to the great majority of both men and women. For about one man in ten, however, the sexual drive is more like a woman's, more person-related (and seeking greater intimacy) than time-related. Similarly, perhaps one in ten women have a biologically driven sexual urge like that of men.

Male and female sexual drives

It will be clear from the above discussion that men are interested in initiating sex when their drive is high. Women are not generally keen to initiate sex (although in some women the desire is in the male pattern), but most women are ready to be aroused if the circumstances are right. A woman's sexual drive, as confirmed by recent research, is more in the nature of being ready to become sexually aroused rather than having a proactive desire to initiate the sexual act even if she is experiencing sexual fantasies of some kind or observing some situation or person that she finds erotic. This is something that men find very hard to understand, since they tend unrealistically to expect to see a male pattern of sexual interest, and a similar wish to initiate, in their female partners.

Male and female sexual approaches

This difference causes some problems in relationships in which one partner expects the other to have a sexual drive exactly like their own. A man with a strong biological sex drive driven by testosterone may find it very hard to understand why his woman partner doesn't feel like sex at the same time as he does. There may be all sorts of reasons for this, such as pressure of responsibilities or even resentment of him, but the man would often feel that, whatever the difficulties, a good sexual experience would help to solve them. The woman might give in and have sex because he wants it, but this might then store up greater problems for the future, when sex becomes the main focus for disagreements between them. A simple summary of the differences between men and women could be that men come to a good relationship through sex, whereas women come to sex through a good relationship.

The sexual experience itself

Differences are found too in the emphasis on the sexual experience itself. For men this is usually a penis–driven event, with the most important part of it being the quality of the physical relationship, a good erection, a good orgasm for both partners and mutual satisfaction. For women this is partly true, but in many cases the most important part of the experience is the emotional response of both partners, and sex is valued because it increases their closeness, intimacy and understanding, strengthening their relationship.

The need for confidence and the need for trust

In the same way, the man in a sexual relationship needs to feel confident in order to have an erection, while a woman needs to feel a sense of trust in the partner to relax into the situation. Most men tend to find it hard to understand their female partner's attitude to sex, just as they may find it hard to communicate with her in non-sexual areas. Women know more about men's attitudes, because men are more 'up-front' about sex and sexual drives, but again women will often reject some of the more crude and obvious approaches.

What about same-sex relationships?

There may be fewer such misunderstandings in same-sex relationships, and the partners are usually more in tune on sexual matters. However, we have seen a number of both gay and lesbian couples where the frequency of sex was a big issue, and where one partner was much more insistent on sex than the other. The same-sex relationship therefore does not provide a panacea, but by and large these sexual misunderstandings are less severe in same-sex relationships, although they may not necessarily be any easier to talk about.

How can we live more comfortably together?

We will be discussing in Chapter 7 how to deal with the misunderstandings created by these kind of situations, and how men and women can live more comfortably and amicably with the differences between them.

Arousal and orgasm

Sexual arousal is not the same thing as sexual drive or desire, and although it is unusual to have arousal without drive in men, in women this can often be the case. In men, sexual arousal is centred around the erection of the penis. This is usually quite obvious to the man, and may lead to a strong desire for sexual release. In women, sexual arousal is felt as moistness or wetness in the vagina, often with some tingling, swelling or enlargement of the clitoris and a general feeling of increased bodily sensitivity to touch. It can therefore be less obvious to her, and also to her partner, that she is aroused, whereas arousal is very obvious in the man. In good sexual interaction, the arousal of one partner is a stimulus for the other to get aroused; but where there are misunderstandings, the man may assume that his partner is feeling exactly the same way as he is, and he may 'jump the gun' and start the sexual interaction prematurely.

Communicating about sex

It is not unusual to encounter problems in sexual communication between partners. The woman may say that she is ready for sex, meaning that she is emotionally turned on by the situation but not yet physically aroused, while the man may take this as a signal to go ahead with sex. If they are to have a mutually satisfying sexual experience, it is necessary for the woman to let her partner know how 'turned on' she is sexually, and if it is not clear he should make the effort to find out. It is in this kind of situation that it is very

65

important for communication to be clear and understood by both partners.

Differences in orgasm

In men orgasm is accompanied by ejaculation, as well as a sense of extreme pleasure, and it is a very obvious event. Women have a very similar muscular response, involving about eight to ten contractions of the muscles around the vagina and clitoris, and a very similar feeling of pleasure, but without an ejaculation as such, although some experts maintain that some women can ejaculate fluid at the time of orgasm. Stimulation in the area of the 'G' spot (an area in the front wall of the vagina) can help a woman reach climax and orgasm. The major difference for men and women is in the 'refractory period'. In men this is a time following orgasm when they are completely unable to be aroused sexually: in young men it may last about twenty minutes, in older men up to twelve hours. Women do not have this refractory period, and many women are able to go on to have multiple orgasms if the sexual stimulation continues for long enough. In a way, this equalises the sexual experience, with men having the stronger desire for it, while women can have a more intense experience.

Spontaneity

The problems caused by any differences between male and female sexual drives and arousal are most acute in the situation where sex might or might not happen. Much is made in romantic fiction, and even more in sexually explicit fiction, about the moment when a couple realise that they both seem to want sex at the same time. This idea of spontaneity is taken up by the readers and seems to have taken over as the ideal of how sex *should* be. Couples who have what to them had previously seemed to be a quite satisfactory sex life, become worried because they read in the media about spontaneous passion and the satisfaction it brings, and if they don't experience it they think that there is something wrong with their own sex lives. The situation is made worse by the emphasis in the media on simultaneous orgasm. Couples, and more usually the man, become upset because they are not having mutual, simultaneous orgasms. Again, they wrongly assume that they are missing out on something that almost everyone else is experiencing, and they can blame either their own 'inadequate technique' or their partner's lack of response. In reality, it is probably a minority of couples who have mutually spontaneous sex and regular simultaneous orgasms.

Expectations

Relationships in their early stages

From what we were saying above, it should be clear that expectations of what should happen in a sexual experience are both important to the individuals and quite problematic. The man's insistence on the central importance of sexual intercourse is not always accepted by the woman, but she may not be able to say this openly for many reasons. Firstly the man may take offence because he feels that his sexual ability is being questioned, and part of his self-esteem may be based on his perception that he is a good lover. Then the woman, at least in the early stages of the relationship, may be afraid that unless she is enthusiastic about sex she may lose her partner. Even when the sexual side is going well, there is usually a time when one or the other partner goes off sex for a time, and they may feel that this is disastrous, and that it threatens the relationship. This may be more of a problem for young couples, where neither partner is experienced, and their ideas of what sex should be like are taken from books, the internet, television or their friends' (often boastful) accounts.

Sex in a steady relationship

Here the problem is still to do with expectations, but the expectations may be different from those in the early part of the relationship. The couple may have lost the first flush of passion and be settling down to a more steady sexual pattern. They don't have the same unrealistic ideas that often characterise the early relationship. There is now some understanding on both sides of the other's needs. However, other factors may come in to affect the sexual side, and sex may have to be fitted in with work patterns, sport, children's homework, house cleaning and bedtime routines. Ideally this leads to a regular but varied pattern of sexual interaction, which is accepted by both partners, and this may be punctuated by unusually good experiences after a night out or on holiday. However, in some couples where the issue has not been discussed, there may be serious misunderstandings and arguments.

How to deal with sexual problems

When sexual difficulties arise in couples, it is usually helpful to discuss the problem, and often a clearer understanding of the other person's point of view will solve it. However, this discussion should not be overdone, and sometimes to spend hours discussing 'us and our sexual problems' becomes a problem in itself. The more some couples discuss it the more it seems to take over their lives, and a secondary sexual 'problem' is created which is even more difficult to solve. As ever, the solution is one of compromise, and the couple may have to leave the discussion and just act instinctively, rather than try to find a definitive solution. Further advice will be found in Chapter 7, which covers the management of sexual problems in couples.

How to avoid the expectation trap: good enough sex

The new couple will sooner or later find their own balance in the area of sexual adjustment. The concept of 'good enough sex' is one that has not been used much outside our own clinics, although the phrase 'good enough parents' is widely used in family therapy in trying to help parents to be more relaxed in bringing up their children. This helps them to get away from the anxieties about being inadequate in their parenting, and emphasises the fact that there is probably no such thing as ideal parents, but most parents do a fairly good job. The same concept could be applied to the sexual relationship that couples build up. 'Good enough sex' is something that most couples experience, and if sex is not a great problem for them it is probably not worth worrying about.

What about orgasm?

This 'good enough' question is particularly important in the area of orgasm. Sometimes the man is so keen that his partner should achieve a good orgasm, ideally at the same time that he himself does, that it can become an area of conflict for the couple. Many women find it difficult to achieve orgasm, and some need extra stimulation, perhaps using a vibrator, to do so. In fact, many women are quite satisfied with non-orgasmic sex, and value the closeness and the emotional intimacy that it brings, without worrying about a climax. The man, however, may have the expectation that all women should experience a simultaneous orgasm with their male partner, and that if this doesn't happen there must be something wrong either with her or with his technique. The couple should be encouraged to settle for either a non-orgasmic but satisfactory sexual relationship, or for the woman experiencing orgasm in some other way, for example with manual stimulation or a vibrator.

The effect of earlier experiences

Most people in a sexual relationship have had earlier experiences which are relevant. These may be actual sexual events, they may simply involve talking or reading about sex, or they may be non-sexual experiences which bear on the sexual life of the couple, such as one partner suffering a humiliation or a disappointment in the past.

The first sexual experience

This often has a profound influence on the person, and it may lead to a lifelong fear of sex or, alternatively, a lifelong addiction to it. Sex will hopefully be with consent, and should then not lead to any adverse consequences. However, it is very unusual for the first sexual experience to be completely trouble-free; there may be pain for the woman, and often the man will ejaculate prematurely. If the couple then go on to develop a regular sex life, these problems will usually quickly resolve themselves. Sometimes, however, there may be a rejection by one of the partners following this event, and the rejected partner may develop a fear around sex in the future.

Traumatic sexual experiences

More severe problems can arise following a first sexual experience which is non-consensual, for example when force is used, maybe amounting to a rape. Here the woman may develop a true post-traumatic stress reaction, and this can cloud her sexual life for many years to come. Even worse is the situation where the experience is in the form of sexual abuse of an underage partner, whether male or female. The abuse victim may not even realise at first that anything wrong is happening, but soon the realisation will dawn, and usually the experience is emotionally traumatising from the beginning. It is for some victims (but not all) impossible to overcome the inhibitions and fears that follow a traumatic sexual experience without professional help; this may be necessary not only for the victim but also for their partner, who is sometimes described as the 'second victim'. Therapy is not easy in this situation, but results tend to be better if there is a combination of individual therapy for the victim and couple therapy for both partners.

The influence of other earlier relationships

Most people, however, are not in their first sexual relationship, and there may be many memories and regrets, even nostalgia, relating to earlier partnerships, perhaps when the person was a teenager. There is often a feeling that the present relationship is not as good as the earlier one, and this may lead to tension and quarrels over apparently unconnected issues.

Unusual sexual needs

Some people, particularly men, may have things that turn them on sexually other than having sex with another person.

It may be more exciting for such people to cross-dress, to wear leather, to be beaten by their partner or to ask their partner to do other things like wearing specific kinds of clothing or to suck their toes as part of their sexual arousal routine. This is usually more of a problem for the partner than for the man himself. When the needs have not been disclosed in the early part of the relationship, it is often a cause for a serious reconsideration of the commitment of the woman to the man. He may very well wish that she would simply accept him as he is with his special needs, but she might find herself turning off her partner, and she may ask him to give it up for her sake.

How to cope with unusual sexual needs

If a good relationship exists apart from the special needs, it may be possible to negotiate some sort of compromise between them, for example to use the leather gear during sex on some occasions and to have normal intercourse on others. Giving reassurance about how common many of these sexual preferences are can help, and may encourage partners to explore other options that may be fulfilling to them as well. However, in some cases the problem is insoluble, and the couple end up separating.

Making too much of sex

Sometimes a relationship begins with a very strong sexual attraction and the couple want this to continue indefinitely.

However, the sexual urge and sexual satisfaction are not always able to be guaranteed in the longer term, and the couple may be disappointed that, after some time, their sexual life is not as exciting or satisfying as before. One answer to this problem is to try to re-establish the exciting sexual life that has been lost, and with help from a therapist this is often possible. However, it may be more sensible to rethink the priorities within the relationship, and to build a better general relationship together, including non-sexual joint interests, without relying on the 'glue' of sexuality to keep it together.

Sex and relationships: how they interact with each other

In some ways sex can be seen as a continuation of the general relationship in a different mode. The way partners interact in bed will often be similar to the way they interact in their life together. So a man who is quite dominant in general will often be dominant in the same way in the sexual setting. A woman who likes to be looked after and prefers to avoid conflict would be expected to be somewhat similar in bed. This is fine as long as it suits both partners and does not cause conflict. However, the conflicts which a couple have in their general life together will often resurface in the sexual situation, and competitiveness in the bedroom may prevent sex or make it very problematic. In trying to resolve the sexual problem it is usually helpful to look at your general relationship, and improvements in that can be reflected in the sexual situation.

Stresses leading to sexual problems

Many couples have quite a stressful life together, and this may be reflected in their sexual life. It is well known that stress of any sort can interfere with sexual function, causing loss of erection and lack of arousal. However, this is multiplied when the main cause of stress is the relationship with the sexual partner him/herself. One of the commonest causes of sexual difficulties is the continuation of arguments into the bedroom, or one partner continuing to feel resentful of the other when trying to have sex together.

Sexual problems causing stress

On the other side of the coin, there are couples who have had a very good relationship until a sexual problem arises, perhaps through a physical illness or an outside stress. Here the presence of the sexual problem leads to a worsening of the general relationship, and the couple spend their time arguing about sex, including the question as to why it isn't happening, whose fault it is, or how to put the situation right.

The 'kiss and make up' situation

Sometimes, however, the couple have found that having an argument can be helpful to their sex life. They kiss and make up after it, and then go on to have good sex. This may be a good way to enhance their sex life, but the problem is that the arguments may spiral out of control, and lead to either physical fights or prolonged resentments which then prevent sex from happening. It is a high-risk situation, which some couples can handle for long periods, but there is always the chance that the arguments may become intractable and lead to serious violence, and ultimately divorce (see Chapters 7 and 9).

The good 'team' who don't get together physically

There are other couples who have a very good general relationship, sharing the same ideals and politics, working together to run the house or the family, who never seem to find time or motivation for sex. They are good team players, but don't seem to have the passion to get together sexually. It is often difficult to break out of this pattern in a marriage, and they may have to accept that sex is not a high priority for them.

Practical difficulties in the bedtime routine

We have often heard from couples who have a poor sexual relationship that they have developed a routine in which they don't go to bed at the same time, or that one partner is asleep when the other gets to bed. You may think that this is because one or both of them wants to avoid sex, but it may also arise from circumstances such as one partner needing to get up early or being more tired in the evening. It is always worth considering a change in the routine, not necessarily every night, in order to leave the possibility for sex to happen.

Worrying about the children

Another practical difficulty is the inability to 'close the bedroom door'. One or both partners are concerned about the welfare of their children, and find it difficult to stop listening for them in order to devote themselves to sex. It often takes a full discussion of the issues between the partners to make it possible to exclude the children physically from the bedroom during sexual activities, or to stop one or both partners worrying about them during sex. The same problem sometimes occurs in relation to other relatives or friends staying in the house, and some couples have even had the problem with dogs monopolising the bedroom and seeming by their presence to prevent sex between the partners.

Sharing a double bed

In the same practical area there are sometimes difficulties with how to share a bed. One partner may be prone to move over to the other's side of the bed, or they may fight over the control of the sheets and duvet. The double bed is a good model for the sharing of territory in a relationship, and the struggles which can take place will often reflect other areas of conflict in the non-sexual life of the couple.

Taking each other for granted

Sometimes a couple who have been together for many years feel that they know each other so well that there is no need for much communication about the relationship. This can lead to difficulties when something happens, such as one partner getting another job, one of the children developing an illness or outside stresses such as difficult neighbours. The same kind of problem may result from one of the transitions in the 'family life-cycle' (see Chapter 1). The couple may not discuss their mutual concerns, but the problem may show itself in a weakening of their sexual life, and they may then drift into a state of increasing isolation from each other. In many of these couples a simple discussion will increase their mutual understanding, and may help them with the sexual problem.

What does sex do for the relationship?

The significance of sex within a partnership may differ greatly. For some it is a means of getting emotionally close, an expression of their love for each other. For others it is more of a recreation, some fun that they can have together. This is less important if both partners are of the same mind, but in some couples there is a conflict about the significance of sex, as to whether it expresses feelings of love or simply satisfies desires.

CASE EXAMPLE

An example of the difference in attitude to sex is illustrated by the case of Robert (48) and Fiona (45). He was a company director who had moved from a very active role as chief executive officer to a more advisory one as chairman, and she was running a small business. Their children were all over twenty and away from home. He had been upset by her lack of interest in sex, and was almost ready to believe that she could be unfaithful. The real problem was caused by their different attitudes to the sexual relationship. To her it was a form of indoor recreation, which was the 'icing on the cake' of an otherwise good relationship. To him it was an expression of their deep love for each other, and the fact that she could take it so lightly upset him greatly. In therapy they realised their problem and she was able to take the situation more seriously, while he helped her by donating some money, in her exclusive control, to help her with the business (a sign of his increased trust in her). They ended with a more satisfactory sex life and a more peaceful relationship.

Sex-related irritability

In many younger couples there is tension between the partners when sex has not happened for some days or weeks, and this may be expressed by the man getting irritable. When sex takes place, the man's irritability will often decrease, and if this is the main cause of conflict, then conflict will also be reduced after sex.

The art of persuasion

Some men, particularly those who have a higher sexual drive than their partner, will assume that being kind or generous to the partner (bringing chocolates or roses) will make her more interested in sex. This does not always work, particularly if the ways he chooses to be generous do not mean very much to her. For example, a man may buy his wife expensive presents in the hope that she will find his advances more acceptable, and not realise that what she really wants is more discussion and more help with the children. Her motivation for sex may be increased if he begins to take her worries seriously, gives her practical help and psychological support, and treats her more like a real partner than a sex object.

Some suggestions for improvement in the sexual relationship

It is usually helpful to talk about the sexual side of the relationship if there seem to be difficulties (see above). Certainly it is better to talk about the problem than not talk about it. If something like this becomes a silent area in the communication, there is usually an increase in the severity of the problem.

Be clear and specific

In talking about it, the rules of good communication should be used. Rather than emphasising the complaints it is better to centre on the ways that the situation might be improved (see Chapter 5). So, if the woman feels that the man is not giving her the things that she needs, it is better for her to ask for them specifically rather than complaining that he doesn't understand her. The requests, from either partner, should be detailed and specific, and very clear to the person who is receiving them. So, to say 'I want you to be more loving' is not an ideal request, whereas 'I would like us to hug and kiss like we used to do' helps the partner to know what is needed.

Overcoming inhibitions about discussing sex

It is quite difficult for many couples to talk about the sexual area, and it may require some skill and confidence to raise it. Most individuals are quite sensitive about their sexual attractiveness, and about their level of knowledge or technique, and it is a difficult feat to raise the topic with a partner when there are problems. Perhaps it is safer to compliment the partner when it goes well, rather than to criticise when it goes badly, and after the compliments to say what might improve the experience next time. Some couples have managed to communicate about it non-verbally, for example by taking the other person's hand during intimate moments and putting it where it feels better. Alternatively, the couple can develop a way of signalling non-verbally, by squeezes or caresses, when they like something, and by pulling away a little or making gentle sounds if something is not so welcome.

Further measures to be taken

If it becomes clear that they cannot communicate without either irritability or misunderstandings, the couple may decide that it is necessary to consult a sexual therapist or counsellor. These professionals will help them to communicate without misunderstandings, and respect the sensitivity that both partners have about the sexual areas.

Suggestions for self-help

Whether they do it alone or with the help of the professionals, most couples can be helped by using an approach which we will be covering in Chapter 7. This is based partly on the teachings of the pioneers of sex therapy, Masters and Johnson, but also utilises the principles of communication and negotiation that we will be describing in Chapter 5. The basis of it is the return to a kind of prolonged foreplay (sensate focus), which helps the couple to become comfortable with each other's bodies while not feeling under pressure to perform sexually. It can be enhanced by learning a new and more positive way of communicating about sex, and by understanding the differences between individuals' responses both in sex and in the general relationship.

Key Points

- Men and women are different in terms of brain function, psychology, language use and coping abilities.
- There are also differences in sexual drive, sexual responsiveness, sexual arousal and orgasm.

- Men are testosterone driven whereas women are more aroused by intimacy, relationship factors and emotions.
- Sexual communication is not easy, with misunderstandings happening easily on both sides.
- Expectations can be unrealistic, especially on the male side.
- Earlier experiences, especially traumatic ones, can affect the individual's sexual response.
- Sexual and non-sexual parts of the relationship can influence each other.
- Talking about the sexual side can help, but it should not be too prolonged or intense.
- Non-verbal communication can often be more helpful.
- Professional help may be needed in more difficult situations.

PART TWO

WHAT TO DO ABOUT IT

4

Tackling relationship problems

Introduction

This chapter is concerned with the various types of relationship problem that couples experience, and offers some general suggestions on how to deal with them. Chapters 5 and 6 will go into much more detail as to the methods you might use to help yourselves.

How to define a relationship problem

Relationship problems are not very easy to define, and sometimes it may be impossible for a couple to agree whether there is a problem or not. If you both agree that there is a problem, you can start to work on it, but if only one of you recognises the problem, it is difficult to make any progress at all. The ironic thing is that if you can't agree whether you have a relationship problem, that is usually a relationship problem in itself!

Who notices that something is wrong?

It is more often the woman who identifies a problem, and it has been found, for example, that women are more likely than men to initiate a referral to a relationship counsellor. Men often prefer to find medical or other kinds of active solutions to problems, and are more impatient than women with the slower and more reflective approach of counselling.

How do you get your partner interested in problem solving?

This book, of course, is about relationships, and the ideas are more likely to be helpful if both partners are working together to solve their problems. If you are reading it alone, think about ways in which you could get your partner interested in the ideas presented here. Some possible strategies are:

- Tell them about the book and discuss some of the ideas.
- Get them to look at the 'key points' at the end of each chapter.
- Read the book together and try some of the exercises (the ideal solution).
- If all else fails, try the paradoxical technique of saying 'You shouldn't really read it because you wouldn't understand.'

Attack and counter-attack

Many couples with problems are in a constant state of war. This is in some ways the most familiar type of relationship problem, as seen on stage, in movies and in novels (e.g. *Who's Afraid of Virginia Woolf?*). In this kind of 'symmetrical' relationship it often seems that it is more important to win the argument than to preserve the relationship or to ensure the welfare of other family members.

The battle lines are drawn up

The battles between spouses or partners should not of course amount to a state of war, but there are some common factors. The use of language – *'his behaviour is totally selfish', 'she is completely unreasonable', 'I'm a victim of his sadistic cruelty'* – seems to indicate that there is no chance for any truce between the two partners. Often there are also physical fights between them, and as we will see in Chapter 9, these can become very dangerous, especially for the woman. It often seems that there is no room in this situation for tenderness, sympathy or reconciliation.

How to overcome the stalemate

Many couples in this situation end up getting divorced, but this is not inevitable, and if they can get out of the war zone they may be able to see that the relationship is worth preserving. The problem is that each partner sees him/herself as the victim, and the other as the persecutor.

So each partner sees their own behaviour as 'just acting in self-defence', while the other partner interprets the same behaviour as unprovoked aggression.

Create a demilitarised zone?

It might be possible with some thought to find the middle ground, an area where both of you can approach, waving a white flag, and talk about issues without fighting. As we suggest in Chapter 5, you might try having a timer going for the discussion, and agree to go to different rooms at the end. Alternatively, you might agree to break off as soon as the discussion gets too heated and start again at another time.

Kiss and make up?

On the other hand, these battles do not necessarily last for long, and the couple may be very loving and positive in-between battles. The battles may then be a preliminary to sex, in the 'making up phase', although the danger is that the rows may also go on for too long, so that sex becomes impossible because of the continual hostility.

How to Break the Cycle

- One possibility is to leave a pause between speakers, so as to reduce the risk of 'shooting from the hip' and making a counter-attack.

- Another way is to try and see the other's point of view, for example by deliberately swapping roles (he takes over her arguments and she takes over his, as detailed in Chapter 6).
- A third possible way is to start communicating indirectly – by telephone, by texting or by email.
- A fourth possibility, which is very good if you can achieve it, is to realise that underneath the bitterness is a great deal of sadness, so that you should sympathise with your partner rather than attacking them.
- Or, as a last resort, maybe you could stop talking about your differences altogether, and just get on with life.

None of these are guaranteed to be successful, but they may succeed in breaking the deadlock, and if any kind of truce can be called it may be possible to get on with a more constructive discussion.

Getting help, informally or professionally

Sometimes a third party may be able to act as referee, and stop the partners from attacking each other: the danger is, however, that the third person may be seen as being biased and one partner or both may begin to dislike them.

Ministers, rabbis, imams or fellow members of a religious congregation, who are seen by both as being impartial, may be able to help. However, if it can be arranged, and is acceptable to both partners, a referral to a relationship counselling service may be the best hope of finding someone who is unbiased and able to help with the communication.

Once you have a truce, what then?

When the truce has started, the couple have to agree how to continue their dialogue. It is important to avoid starting the arguments again, so a change of direction is needed, in which you suspend your belief that your partner is to blame, and act as if you were both allies trying to improve your relationship. Each of you has to see that the other is a friend rather than an enemy, at least for the time being, and tune in to their distress rather than their faults.

Get away from the victim/persecutor mindset

There is a common problem that almost all attack–attack couples share, and this is the way in which each partner thinks of him/herself as the victim and the partner as the persecutor. You might have to ask yourself the question: 'What is it that I am doing that might be making matters worse?' It is a hard thing to do, but it underlines the relevance of the phrase 'the only person you can change is yourself' (see Chapter 5).

Change the way you communicate

Having made the shift to taking some responsibility for the problems, the partners then have to change the way they communicate. There are several ways of communicating more effectively, and they are dealt with in more detail in Chapter 5. In summary:

- One approach is reciprocity negotiation: the partners state their wishes rather than complaints, and try to do deals, in which they give each other what they want in exchange for the other doing something equivalent for them.
- The other way to solve the stalemate is communication training, in which the couple learn to understand the other's point of view, to make positive comments, to speak from the 'I' position and to think in terms of the future rather than the past.

What if the arguments come back?

There will no doubt be many times when a couple who have once been at war find themselves slipping back into the old conflict. The only way to avoid this is for both of you to be aware of your own contribution to the escalating conflict, and to pull back from the brink. It takes two to have a fight, and, in this situation, if one partner decides not to fight you may both be able to reduce the conflict. As we said, it is vital for both partners to observe the truce for long enough to create a new kind of dialogue.

Attack and withdrawal

This is a variation on the attack–attack scenario. Here only one partner is on the attack, and the other one withdraws, either emotionally or by getting out of the situation. This is in some ways easier for both to tolerate than the attack–attack scenario, and less likely to result in a physical fight, but it can be very frustrating for the active partner, and very wearing for the one who withdraws.

A 'machine gun and a fort': siege warfare

As in the attack–attack situation each partner feels that they are in the right. They may use the same kind of words as the attack–attack couple, for example: *'She's unreasonable and her attacks are out of proportion to the problem'*, or *'I can't get him to respond, he goes into a sulk and it gets very lonely and frustrating'*. However, it is difficult to find a solution to the problem, because thanks to the withdrawal, the couple can never get to the point of discussing it at any length. It is often a bit like a battle between a machine gun and a fort. The person who is attacking goes heavily into criticism and complaint, while the other remains quiet, noncommittal and defensive, and appears to be waiting for the storm to 'blow over'.

How to get out of the stalemate

The attacking partner has to realise that the criticisms are not achieving their goal, and somehow reduce them. Their criticisms are often justified, but simply repeating them does not seem to produce an effect.

In the meantime the defending partner has to be prepared to come out and be a little more receptive, which may be possible if he or she can begin to understand that the partner finds their withdrawal painful.

Communicate and negotiate

Again, as in the attack–attack situation, the couple may be able to use some negotiating or communicating skills as outlined in Chapter 5, and thus be able to make better use of the complaints and wishes expressed by the critical partner. The case presented here is an example of how a couple might use reciprocity negotiation for a problem of 'attack and withdraw'.

CASE EXAMPLE

Gordon (50) was married to Bertha (48). Their two children had left home, Bertha was a homemaker, and their relationship problem involved her constant criticisms and his defensive excuses. It mainly centred around his late-ness in returning from work, and her annoyance about it. She would usually criticise him for about thirty minutes without listening to his answers, and then eventually he would explain irritably why he was late. In therapy they reached a compromise in which he agreed to telephone her to give her his expected time of arrival. He would then stick to this as far as possible, and when he got in he would tell her what he had been doing. She promised to listen to him in silence for ten minutes and then 'give a soft answer'. This worked, to the extent that their arguments diminished considerably, and incidentally his sexual desire for her, which had been very low, recovered to its previous level.

A time-limited trivial argument?

Communication and negotiation is not always possible, and another way around the problem is for the withdrawing partner to become more assertive and argue back. This may be difficult, and feel dangerous to the withdrawing partner, but it may be possible in the form of a time-limited argu-ment on a trivial issue (see the exercise in Chapter 6) which gives the couple a chance to 'agree to differ' at the end and both withdraw after the discussion. This then leads to the withdrawing partner feeling less persecuted and listening more seriously to the wishes of the 'attacker'.

But won't this just lead to total war?

It is true that sometimes when the withdrawing partner becomes more assertive there is a risk of greater conflict, at least for a time, but in due course the couple learn that it is possible to be assertive and not enter an endless conflict. The whole purpose of the 'trivial argument' approach is that the couple can argue and then terminate the arguments, often by 'agreeing to differ'. In any case, the fact that they have been able to change is an indication to them that things don't have to be the same forever, and that they can do something about the situation.

'You're bossy!' 'No, I'm just being responsible.'

The next type of couple is also quite familiar in literature and the media. The more cautious, or 'bossy', partner has a need to feel that things are under control. This leads them to worry about anything the other partner does which seems to be less carefully thought out than they would have liked. The more carefree partner, on the other hand, thinks that the cautious partner is being too fussy and controlling, and treats the whole situation either as a joke or with an irritable response.

Boundaries and territory

The problem is really one of dispute over boundaries and territory. The cautious and responsible partner is treating the carefree one as if they were a child, and of course a parent has to be responsible for the behaviour of the child. However, the carefree partner wants to be independent as an adult, and resents the idea of the cautious partner intruding over the boundary and controlling them.

Who is right?

The central issue, as to whether the carefree partner is really irresponsible, or whether the cautious partner is being intrusive and unnecessarily anxious, is not that important. Each partner would probably maintain that they are right and the other is wrong. The kind of conversation often heard in these couples goes along the lines of: *'Why do you have to treat me like a child?' 'I only do it because you act like a child'*. There is often no solution if they continue to hold these opposite views, and the situation develops into a stalemate, with each partner recruiting allies from among their friends and relatives, as in: *'My wife treats me like a child, she doesn't understand me'* and *'My husband is totally irresponsible, he spends money like water'*.

How to find a solution

This is not at all easy. Ideally the couple should sit down and discuss their plans, perhaps on the basis of a timed discussion, in which each agrees to close the subject after a set period of maybe ten minutes (see Chapter 5). In doing so they may reach a compromise which is acceptable to both.

This might leave them with an agreement about how much risk it is acceptable for the carefree partner to take without being criticised.

Redrawing the boundaries

The couple may in this way be able to reach an agreement dividing up the territories and deciding who is responsible for which areas of their life together. However, this will always be in danger of being broken if the cautious partner believes that something is being done that is risky. Gradually the more carefree partner may learn that some courses of action are likely to trigger a 'responsible' reply, and begin to avoid them. The most lasting solution is if both partners can negotiate the areas which they take the lead in, and respect the other's areas of control (see Chapters 5 and 6).

Planning versus flexibility

This is a variant of the previous relationship problem, and in this version one partner likes to plan life well ahead, while the other tends to be more ready to make snap decisions. This can cause difficulties when there is a clash between the plans of the planner and the wishes of the impulsive partner. In tackling the problem both partners should try to recognise that they themselves don't have the answers to all the problems of life, and that the other person can contribute something. If they can agree on a compromise which is bearable to them both, this can be a workable solution.

However, it will not work for all situations, and more radical solutions may have to be sought, such as the following:

Planned and non-planned days

One of these is the possibility of having planned days and non-planned days in alternation, each orchestrated by one partner while the other goes along with the regime. Both partners then have the reassurance that they have a day to look forward to which is to their own liking, and therefore put up with the days that do not suit them so well. Ironically, of course, the impulsive partner will have to engage in this form of planning in order to have a non-planned day.

CASE EXAMPLE

Bernard (47) and Luisa (38) have two sons, aged 9 and 7. Luisa's constant complaint is that Bernard doesn't plan things for himself or the family, but likes to see what the weather forecast says before deciding on the activity for the day. She wants their life to be more planned, and in particular would like to entertain more and go out to see friends more. He loves to go to greyhound racing, the boys also enjoy this sport, and he and the boys do this regularly. However, Luisa finds it boring, and doesn't usually go with them. In therapy they negotiated one evening a month when they would all go greyhound racing with friends (which satisfied them both because it was a good outing for him and also involved friends, which pleased her). They also agreed to have a diary session in which they would both plan regular dinners with friends, but leave some weekend days free for unplanned family activities.

Possessiveness and the question of fidelity

Most couples work on the basis that they are in a sexually exclusive relationship. It is generally understood by them both that any infidelity will be viewed negatively by the other partner, and if such outside relationships occur they will usually be kept secret from the partner. Some people are naturally more possessive than others, and some partners become uneasy when their partner is, as they see it, too open and familiar with friends or colleagues. This may cause difficulties for both partners, without leading to jealousy as such (see Chapter 8), and can be dealt with quite successfully by discussion.

Open relationships

Some couples have an understanding that the relationship can be an open one sexually. This can take the form of 'swinging', in which they go to parties where there is an expectation that the couples there will exchange partners sexually. It may also take the form of an agreement that each partner may have outside relationships without telling the other. This 'open relationship' policy seems to be more common among gay male couples than either heterosexuals or lesbians. In whatever setting, it is likely to be somewhat risky, and increases the possibility that one or other partner will find someone who suits him or her better than the existing partner. It is also something which usually appeals to one partner (often male) more than the other, and would have to be carefully negotiated between them before they undertake to meet other couples for sexual activities.

It has the possible advantage of overcoming the problem of the relationship becoming sexually 'stale' and the partners remaining with each other for the wrong reasons. However, the constant change of partners may become boring to them in the same way as if they stayed together exclusively.

The following illustrates the management of a conflict involving sex with other partners.

CASE EXAMPLE

Steve and Adam (both in their thirties) came into therapy seeking advice on whether there was a way to keep their relationship together. The couple had been in a monogamous relationship for their first four years. Adam recently shared that he had sought one-night relationships whilst away on business trips. The couple now spoke about this on most evenings and this stopped closeness and intimacy occurring when they retired into bed. Early into therapy Steve asked Adam why this was happening and he heard a clear message from Adam that as they no longer undressed together and washed each other in the shower that he felt undesirable and needed to know that other men still found him attractive and sexy. The couple agreed to refrain from speaking about this matter after 7 p.m. Adam agreed that he would offer to strip for Steve twice a week and Steve thanked Adam for the offer, agreeing to encourage him to keep doing so until nude when he noticed that he was getting aroused by the strip. Steve spontaneously mentioned that it would be fun to share his pleasure from seeing his partner undressed and on some occasions would make it unambiguous that he would like to make love with his partner now that he was nude. In return, Adam confirmed that he would find this 'horny' and he would not seek sexual intimacy with another man whilst on business trips.

Jealousy

This can happen whether there is an exclusive relationship or there is an open one. We will be dealing with jealousy at more length in Chapter 8, and so we will only give a brief outline here. Jealousy may be justified, if the partner who has had an outside relationship admits that they have done so. It may, even in these circumstances, still be a very strong feeling (amounting to 'morbid jealousy') and can sometimes lead to violence and even murder; or it may be associated with depression and low self-esteem in the wronged partner. It may, however, be completely unjustified, and that is when it becomes a psychiatric problem, often a form of paranoia. This may happen when there is no evidence that there has been an outside relationship, and the jealous partner becomes obsessed about possible or assumed infidelity.

Possessiveness can be good for the relationship

When two people are in a steady relationship, there is usually an understanding that they will be an exclusive 'item', and not be as open with others as they are with each other. This is something which builds up gradually, starting from the time that they begin to go out together, and gets stronger as the relationship develops. There may be times when this is challenged, for example when one has a very close (but non-sexual) relationship with a friend, a parent or a sibling; this would be a good example of one of the 'triangles' featured in Chapter 6. However, if the partnership is to survive, it is better that the partners should be closer to each other than either of them is to outsiders.

Depression and overprotection

When one partner has suffered a depression, or another kind of mental illness, there may be a marked shift in the dynamics of the relationship. This may even happen gradually over the course of time where there is no illness as such but only a sense that one partner is a bit weaker than the other (see Chapter 8). Either way, the stronger partner may end up taking decisions that should be jointly made, and treating the other as someone who is not fully responsible. This situation is sometimes called the 'doll's house' marriage, after the Ibsen play.

Sometimes there is a conflict as to whether one partner is indeed depressed and in need of therapy. The stronger partner may maintain this quite firmly, while the weaker one may be reluctant to be labelled and treated as ill. It is usually best for the couple to accept the views of the 'weaker' partner as to whether he/she needs treatment or not. In any case, even if treatment is desirable, a reluctant patient is not likely to gain much benefit from it (see the case of Arthur and Mary in Chapter 6).

We will be dealing with this problem in more detail in Chapter 8, but here it may be useful to say that recent research has shown that in couples where one partner is depressed, couple therapy can be just as effective as anti-depressants in helping the depression, and is generally more acceptable to the couple.

Excitement versus peace

People are clearly different from each other in the degree to which they value peace or excitement. Some would be content if there was never any difference in the daily routine of their life, while others become bored if there is nothing going on to interest or amuse them. Generally partners choose each other with a reasonable understanding of the partner's personality and whether they feel they are compatible. However, this does not always happen. When two people who are really incompatible get together it may be because one or both of them has been in a relationship before with someone like themselves and it did not work out. They then seek out a new partner who is completely different from the previous one, and may in the process go out with, and marry, someone who may in the longer term turn out to be incompatible (an example of 'marital fit'; see Chapter 2).

How the couple can overcome their differences and get on better

The quieter partner may feel exhausted by being with the other one for more than a few minutes, and the excitable partner may become bored in about the same time. Somehow they have to find some kind of compromise, and they must realise that in this situation there are no rights and wrongs. Sometimes such couples end up in the divorce court. However, in other cases they learn to live together with their differences, and even value the different insights that they are able to have on life as a result.

Triangles

Life is full of triangular situations, and they may cause difficulties if the partners in a relationship form two points in the triangle, and the third point is a person or an activity. The triangle in this sense is a systemic concept, and simply describes the 'geometry' of a relationship problem.

- The third point of the triangle may be a child, whether biological, step or adopted.

- It may be a parent of one of the partners, or another close relative.
- It may be a friend, or in more serious situations the lover or the ex-wife/husband of one of the partners.
- It may be a sporting activity or a new job which is very absorbing and tiring.

In all these cases the partners have to come to terms with the stresses and strains caused by the triangle. Often the third person is trying to be closer to one of the partners than is comfortable for the other.

How to deal with triangles (see also Chapter 6)

Usually the triangular relationship is one which is accepted by both partners, for example if it is with a mother or friend who is quite close. In some of these cases, however, the relationship is threatened by the triangle, and then the couple must do something about it. The best solution is for them to act as a team in sorting out the difficulty, deciding what is to be done and acting together to solve it.

- For example, the woman whose mother telephones regularly at inconvenient times may ask her to phone at times when the man is not there. It is best that the suggestion of when to telephone comes from the woman in this case, because the man by doing so may antagonise his partner's mother, and this may cause more conflict with his partner.

- The situation with current lovers or ex-partners is more complicated, and we will offer ways of coping with it in Chapters 6 and 11. Usually there is a need for the couple to make some difficult and far-reaching decisions about where each one's loyalty lies and whether the relationship can continue in its present form.

The triangle with a new baby

One of the most common causes of triangular problems is the birth of a baby. Here the mother is naturally wrapped up in loving and caring for the new baby, and the father feels excluded. There may be other pressures, for example from the new mother's own mother, who may take a leading role in baby care and may intentionally or unintentionally exclude the baby's father. If the new mother is also unable or reluctant to be involved in sex this may add to the strains on the couple, and it is at these times that the new father may become involved with a lover, which adds another triangle.

The solution is usually for both partners to be patient and to wait for things to return to normal. They can, however, help by keeping in close communication with each other, and by forming a stronger alliance in the face of outsiders. The involvement of the father in baby care can often be helpful, not only in bringing him closer to the mother, but in developing a parental relationship with the baby (including getting up in the night to feed the baby and change nappies) which otherwise may be rather tenuous until the baby becomes a toddler and the father naturally begins to show more interest.

Outside pressures

In addition to the pressures of family and friends, many couples are subject to pressures from work, travel, neighbours, sports activities and the internet. These often cause problems, which can at times threaten the relationship.

Work problems

This can be a problem for couples where one partner is involved in homemaking and childcare and the other is working. But with the increase in couples who are both working, two sets of work schedules can sometimes cause even more difficulties for their family arrangements. Effectively the two jobs act as two triangles for the couple and they experience competing pressures and loyalties every day. The problems of fitting in with work can affect both childcare and leisure time as a couple, and may be the cause of constant complaints, and sometimes lead to separation.

Possible solutions

The simplest way to deal with the problem of incompatible schedules is for the couple to negotiate a better arrangement. For example, a man whose partner complains about his being unavailable in the evenings could plan to get into work an hour earlier in the morning so as to be home earlier in the evening. Couples who are both working could make more satisfactory arrangements for taking turns in relieving their childminder in the evenings. However, these negotiations are sometimes difficult to manage, and they may have to resort to timetabled discussions under a 'truce' arrangement (see Chapter 5), or get outside help with the problem.

Travel

Travel in connection with work can cause problems for couples, and again the main casualties are either childcare or the couple's leisure activities. If the travelling partner cannot rearrange his/her schedules, the answer may have to be a reduction of the other partner's expectations, or possibly the partners going together for trips abroad.

Periods of work away from home

Sometimes one partner's job unavoidably involves periods

away from home. Perhaps the most familiar example of this is military service, by land, sea or air, which usually entails long periods away from the partner and family, possibly also facing considerable danger. A similar problem is presented by working on a merchant ship, although the physical dangers are not so immediate. It is a predictable source of stress and anxiety for both partners, and to this may be added the anxiety that either partner might meet someone else while they are geographically separated. There is no easy answer to the problems that such couples encounter, and each couple has to make the best adjustment they can to the situation. Regular letters, phone calls and emails can help, and the services themselves are aware of the problems and try through their welfare departments to alleviate the couple's difficulties.

Imprisonment

This has something in common with being in the services, in that the prisoner is separated from the partner and family for periods of time, with only occasional visits allowed. Although the process can be seen as part of the prisoner's just deserts because of the crime committed, the stresses on the partner and the family can be as intense as those experienced by the partners of military personnel. It may be even worse, because of the understandable resentment on the part of the partner towards the person who is in jail. It is unfortunate too that the people who are imprisoned in these circumstances are usually those who have few material resources, and therefore do not have the flexibility to cope with the separation financially. Again there is no easy answer, but regular visiting, letters and phone calls are often helpful in sustaining the relationship until the time comes for release.

Sports activities

These are more often a problem for couples who are at the start of their relationship. One or both partners may have been in the habit of taking part in golf or football, and are often reluctant to give it up for the sake of the new partner. Again, negotiation, with both partners willing to make concessions, will often solve the problem, unless there is an attack–attack or attack–withdrawal situation, in which case they will need to call a truce and discuss the issue carefully.

Neighbours

This is a problem that can test the quality of any relationship, especially if, as often happens, one partner is more upset by the difficult neighbours than the other. As with the triangles mentioned above, the most important consideration is that the partners remain united over the issue, and don't allow themselves to be split. The more sensitive partner may have to delay taking action over the harassment until both partners are convinced that it is the right time. In any case, before they take any action they should carefully think through the consequences – for example retaliation by the aggrieved neighbours. If necessary, the couple may decide to move house in order to preserve their relationship and get away from the difficult situation.

The internet

This is a modern form of relationship stressor, which forms another kind of triangle for the couple. One partner, often the man, becomes obsessed with sitting at the computer for hour after hour, losing sleep, losing interest in the family, losing interest in sex within the relationship and causing stress to his partner. Sometimes the sites are sexual, and it is reported that a surprisingly high proportion of sites visited on the internet are in fact sexually explicit. However, other sites are attractive in other ways, including chat rooms and gambling sites, and are the source of internet compulsions.

The problems are easier to overcome if they are known to both partners, when they can combine their efforts to reduce the time spent on the computer. If, however, the problem is a secret known only to the partner who is using the Net, there is greater difficulty in overcoming it. The problem is the motivation of the user, which is high towards the Net and low towards stopping the activity. Sometimes the situation is discovered accidentally by the partner, and this may lead to a confrontation. Often the Net user will then make promises to give it up, but these may not be kept, and further difficulties lie ahead.

CASE EXAMPLE

Adrian, a writer in his forties, had lived with his partner Susan for fourteen years. He began to use the internet for work purposes, but came across a chat room which dealt with sexual issues, and made contact there with a young prostitute. The sexual relationship with his partner was not very active, mainly through his reluctance, but he visited the prostitute several times and had a more satisfying relationship with her. Susan found out about the internet use via their telephone bill, and became angry, jealous and vindictive, and wanted to know the prostitute's address (Adrian never disclosed this). Adrian was very contrite about the affair, and one day smashed his computer, and continues to work on a tablet. Susan had threatened separation, but actually the couple's sex life became much more active and satisfying after the episode, they decided to get married and their general relationship improved.

General advice on pressures

The problems presented by the pressures mentioned above are common, and usually they can be dealt with in a good relationship without a threat to its stability. However, they may be the last straw in a relationship which is already under stress for other reasons, and the couple, in trying to solve the stressful situation, may endanger their relationship more than they expect.

In general, the way that they deal with the problem can be helpful to the relationship if they use the methods of negotiation and good communication, but if they tackle it by confrontation, blaming or withdrawing, the result may be a separation that neither of them was looking for.

Key Points

- The question of whether a couple have a relationship problem is not easy to determine, especially if one partner says yes and the other says no.
- Some ways are suggested of getting your partner involved in improving the relationship.
- Typical relationship problems include the 'attack–attack' couple, the 'attack–withdraw' couple and the 'bossy–irresponsible' combination.
- Ways of overcoming these problems include reciprocity negotiation and communication training, and having a 'trivial argument'.
- Planning versus impulsiveness, and possessiveness versus openness are two other relationship combinations.
- The solution for these lies partly in redrawing the boundaries around each individual.
- Dealing with 'triangles' and outside pressures can also be helpful in improving relationships.
- Such triangles can include work, geographical separation, problem neighbours, sports activities and excessive use of the computer.
- Awareness of the problems may help couples to find acceptable solutions, which may involve negotiating new kinds of sharing of responsibilities.

5

Self-help: communicating and negotiating

Introduction

In this chapter we have tried to cater for two different situations that you might find yourself in.

- The first and more substantial section is intended for couples who are working together to solve their relationship problems. The exercises and the examples are written under the assumption that there is sufficient cooperation between the two of you for you to try the techniques together and hopefully make successful use of them.

- The second part is written for couples where only one of you will be reading the book, and that person will be trying to improve their relationship working alone. This is of course a harder proposition. However, there is research evidence that one partner, working along the lines we are describing here, can make significant changes.

- At the end is a third section looking at how to maintain the improvements achieved.

How to talk safely together without arguing: timed discussions

If you are having difficulties talking together, this may be adding to your distress over the relationship problems, and in the process further misunderstandings may arise. For example, if one partner tries to talk about the relationship, the other may see this as a ploy to gain attention or to be 'one up'. There are, however, ways to get around this difficulty, and these can often bring you both into a 'safe' kind of discussion about yourselves.

Calling a truce and having a safe discussion

In order to have a safe discussion together, you have to be confident that it will not lead to uncontrollable arguments. Sometimes the only way to do this is to meet with a third person, perhaps a counsellor or mutual friend. However, it can be done by the couple alone, if you observe some fairly simple rules. The first rule is that during the discussion you will maintain a kind of truce, and agree to avoid saying hurtful things. You should also try to use the **rules of good communication** throughout (see the next section, pages 123–124).

Limiting the time for the discussion

To avoid things getting out of control, we have found in our couple therapy clinic that it helps to set a time limit. Couples would be asked to set a timer at the beginning of their talk; in the kitchen this might be a cooking timer, or they might use a stopwatch. For your first 'timed' discussion you should choose a short time, such as ten minutes, divided into two periods of five minutes. One partner should lead the first five-minute period and the other the second.

After the ten minutes, you should then spend some time in separate rooms without talking. You should also agree not to talk about 'us' until the next agreed timed-discussion session.

Come with a prepared script and divide the time

Both partners should come to the first session with a written list of one or two issues they want to discuss during their allotted five minutes, and you should as far as possible stick to these topics in the talk. Your two lists may of course be very different from each other, and it may be that there will have to be a negotiation about which topic can be discussed first. It may also be sensible for you to take turns as to who speaks first session by session, with Partner A starting on the first day and Partner B on the second, so that one partner does not dominate the agenda.

What if one partner is much better at talking than the other?

If the partners are very unequal in their conversational skills, there is a risk that the quieter partner will become swamped by the fluency of the other one, and begin to feel resentment. In this case you should be even more careful about dividing the time evenly, and the more fluent partner should be careful to leave pauses for the other to reply.

What if you begin to argue?

It is vital in the discussion period to try to maintain the truce which has been called, at least for as long as the discussion lasts. One way to reduce the risk of breaking the truce is to try to empathise with your partner – that is, to put yourself into their mind and understand where they are coming from. If the truce cannot be maintained, and you do begin to argue, you should probably end the session early and plan to have another one later. However, an argument in itself may not be a disaster, if you can manage it without losing control. In Chapter 6 we will be giving you some ideas about how to have a good argument and end it on a friendly basis, perhaps by 'agreeing to differ'. You might also try to finish by holding each other in an affectionate way, even though you may not be feeling like it. Either way, the session should end, and you should agree to continue it later, perhaps the next day, when the anger has settled.

Intervals between sessions

Depending upon how well the session has gone, you may decide to have another similar discussion the next day, or after two days, or perhaps delay the repeat discussion for a week or so. Whichever interval you decide on, it must be a joint decision.

As you become more practised at communicating

You will gradually become better at talking without argument or resentment, and the plan will be to extend the time of the sessions up to twenty minutes (still in two ten-minute halves). They could also be held more frequently, such as moving gradually from weekly to daily. For many couples who have relationship problems a daily talk session may be beneficial, as it helps to unburden them from resentments that would otherwise not be mentioned and build up into major irritations. The key is always to keep the discussions friendly and constructive, with a fairly equal sharing of the time between you.

Exercise: Setting Up a Talk Session

- Plan a time when you are not likely to be disturbed. You will need maybe ten minutes if this is your first talk session, but it would be better to leave a bit of leeway after the session.

- Turn off any music, radio or television, and put the phone on 'silent'.
- Set a kitchen timer or stopwatch for two five-minute periods (to give you a changeover time).
- You should both come with a written agenda for one or two things you would like to talk about.
- Try to have an agreement that you will not say hurtful things during the ten minutes.
- Divide the time equally between you.
- Decide who will start with their agenda items.
- Switch over to the other person after five minutes.
- If arguments begin, you could try to end by 'agreeing to differ' at the ten minute deadline, or if they are getting out of hand, you could just stop the session and plan to meet at another time.
- In later sessions you could use communication training or negotiation as the main agenda (see below).
- In later sessions you could extend the time, if you both agree that it is safe to do so, up to twenty minutes at the most.

Good communication (see also Chapter 2, pages 40–44)

This is something which many couples manage without effort. However, those with relationship problems often communicate in a way that makes the problems worse, and it is for them that the next section may be helpful.

The only person you can change is yourself

It's very easy to get into a mindset which assumes that you are a victim and that your partner is unreasonable. It will certainly lead to continued conflict if both of you feel the same about each other. No one, however, has a monopoly on the truth, and there is always room for differences of opinion. The consequence of this idea is to accept that there are two ways of seeing every problem, and you should always try to give your partner the benefit of the doubt. Your partner may also have sensitivities that you haven't noticed, and should be respecting. Ultimately the only person you can change is yourself. When you behave differently your partner will certainly find it easier to change their behaviour too.

Increased toleration

One really important thing to do is to become more tolerant. This means that it is all right to have different opinions, and for you to 'agree to differ' if your partner can't be persuaded that you are right. It also means that there is no shame in the idea of compromising. It is often more fruitful in a relationship for the partners to give up an argument (by agreeing to differ) than to go on until one partner wins or they abandon the argument through exhaustion.

What is good communication?

The general principles of good communication are quite simple, but need to be spelled out. It is important when communicating to say clearly what you mean. You should also show your partner that you understand what they are trying to say (reflective listening) and that you understand their feelings (empathy). It is important to be able to make supportive comments to the partner. It is also part of good communication to have the skills of problem solving.

The general rules of good communication (from Chapter 2)

In Chapter 2 we spelled out ten of the general rules of communication. They are:

- Be brief and simple in what you say
- Leave gaps for your partner to contribute
- Be positive and warm
- If you say something negative, end the sentence with a positive (avoiding the 'sting in the tail')
- Be specific (say what you mean clearly)
- If you don't like something your partner does, it's better to suggest an alternative way of doing it
- Ration discussion of past issues, and concentrate on the present and future

- Stick to the topic and don't drift off into other areas
- If you are talking about your partner, try not to 'mind-read'
- Speak as much as possible from the 'I' position (don't start critical comments with 'you') – see below

CASE EXAMPLE

This couple are in their fifties, both in their second marriage. Brenda is upset because she feels that her husband Claude is insensitive to her feelings. She spends much time criticising him and his insensitivity. He withdraws into a shell (see Chapter 4) and gives defensive answers to her comments. A particular incident comes up again and again, in which some years ago he would spend time talking with an ex-lover while he was in the relationship with Brenda. He said in reply, 'I realise that you were upset when this happened, but I had no intention of hurting you' (he was ending with a defensive comment). She found this unsatisfactory, because she still felt that he was dismissing her distress over the episode. We asked him to put the same sentence the other way around, as 'I had no intention of hurting you, but I realise that you were upset when this happened' (he was ending this time with a sympathetic comment). Brenda found this much more acceptable, even though the same words were being used, because the last part of what he said recognised her distress and indicated that he was taking her more seriously. This is a good example of a 'sting-in-tail' message which has been reworded to make it more positive at the end, and thereby more acceptable. It also shows Claude's increasing awareness of Brenda's sensitivities (see below).

Respecting the other person's sensitivities

In communicating, it is almost always true that if you tread on the other person's sensitivities you will get a negative reaction. This may take the form of an argument or a protest, but it may also be hidden resentment or sadness. It is very important in a relationship, especially one that is fairly new, to be self-aware and to be aware of your partner's sensitivities. A couple who are communicating well will discuss the misunderstandings they have and learn from them.

Isn't it better to be honest?

Couples who have developed a friendly, teasing relationship may get away with 'offending' each other as part of that process, and it can be good fun for both partners. They do, however, always run a slight risk that they may go too far and cause a real hurt unintentionally. There is a similar risk that some people take as the result of a wish to be honest. They say exactly what they feel, regardless of the partner's feelings. While this may be safe enough in the usual run of things, it may cause serious communication problems when the couple are already in difficulties. So a good policy is to think before you speak, and to respect your partner's sensitivities in what you decide to say. Be economical with your honesty.

Sharing feelings

This is something that comes easily to some couples, and, as we said in Chapter 3, it generally comes more easily to women than to men. It is an indication of a good relationship if the two partners can tune in to each other's feelings without difficulty, and be affected by the same kind of situation. To put it more simply, the couple that can laugh at the same things, and cry together about the same things, are likely to have a good and lasting relationship.

Learning to share feelings

It is not easy to learn to tune in to each other's feelings, but one simple exercise is to sit down, perhaps with a timer going, as in the 'talk' exercise, and find out how your partner felt about a recent incident, or a recent film or programme that you have both watched. It should always be done in a spirit of respect, with no criticism if the partner has a different feeling from your own. The advantage of timing the discussion is that it leaves less time for misunderstandings, which might then lead to arguments. It also means that you are not going to feel you have failed if you haven't reached a full understanding of each other's feelings at the end, because there will always be another timed session to follow up your differences. The aim of the exercise is to lead to a greater understanding of the partner, and hopefully a greater degree of tolerance of their feelings and of any differences between them and your own.

Showing empathy

Empathy is a word which is sometimes misunderstood. It isn't necessarily the same as being sympathetic, although they often go together. It really refers to the ability to put yourself in someone else's place and understand how they are feeling. You must be able to feel empathy before you can show it, but it is more difficult to show it. One way of showing empathy is just to repeat what the other person has said in another form of words. For example, if they have just said *'I feel upset and guilty about what I did at the party'*, you might say *'Yes, I can understand that you are feeling upset, it must be quite painful'*. (Note that the empathetic comment doesn't include the word 'guilty', because the first partner might conclude that you think they should feel guilty!) The idea, as above, is to facilitate a continued conversation without necessarily turning yourself into a therapist. It is also an invitation to your partner to show empathy to you in return. Another way to get in touch with the other's feelings is by 'reversed role-play' (see the exercise in Chapter 6, page 160).

Don't mind-read

Empathy is quite difficult to show, and it may sometimes spill over into 'mind-reading', which is really undesirable. It is too easy for one partner to think that they know better than the other one what is in the other one's mind.

'You say you are trying to help but I know that you really want to make me feel bad' is an example of mind-reading. If you are communicating well you should always listen to the other person's explanation of their feelings and respect what they say. People who have had psychotherapy themselves are especially prone to mind-reading, usually because they believe that they have a better understanding of human behaviour than the other partner. As we mentioned before, it is better to remain 'humble' and rely on the other partner to explain how they are feeling rather than indulging in 'mind-reading'.

CASE EXAMPLE

James (52) and his wife Christine (49) had been married for twenty-seven years, and he had suffered from various depressive and phobic symptoms. She had just begun psychotherapy training, and came with him to the first session saying that she felt she had been 'carrying' his depression for twenty years. By this she was implying that he had been 'projecting' his depression onto her unconsciously, and that she had been protecting him from all the stresses that he had avoided through being 'ill'. We discussed this, and he expressed his resentment at being told what was in his mind. It seemed better to leave her interpretation to one side while we worked on her resentment of his behaviour and his wish for more independence. In therapy they achieved a much better balance in their relationship, with her asserting a new independence from him, and him taking much more responsibility for his own stressful episodes in life. The 'mind-reading' with which she started the first session did not feature largely in the subsequent therapy.

Speak as far as possible from the 'I' position

This needs a bit of explanation. It is very easy in a relationship to start most of the things you say with 'You': for example *'You never take time to listen to me'* or *'You make me angry'*. It is much safer, even if perhaps a little boring, to put these ideas across in another way, starting with 'I'. So the first comment might translate as *'I would like you to try to listen more'* (note also the positive and future tone of this re-phrase), and the second as *'I get upset sometimes, and it may be over something you have done'*. The main advantage of starting with 'I' is that your partner can respond to the ideas expressed rather than simply retaliate and get angry in return. It leads to the possibility of dialogue rather than a bitter argument.

Keep to the topic under discussion

It is all too easy in a discussion to raise other issues which are not part of what is being discussed. The new topic may be related to the one being discussed, but is perhaps one which the person who changed the subject feels more strongly about, or feels that they have a better chance of arguing successfully. The problem is that the other partner, the one who wanted to continue talking about the original topic, may feel aggrieved about being cut short. The discussion about the original topic should ideally continue until both partners are satisfied that it has been resolved, or the timer signals the end of the discussion.

Avoid closure and remain flexible

Again, it is very easy to become concerned with winning the argument, or with reaching a conclusion to the discussion. This is not the best approach, because such a conclusion is usually at the expense of one partner, who will feel defeated or at least misunderstood. It is much better to say at the end: *'We'll go on with the discussion another time'*, or to say: *'We can't agree on this, but I respect your right to have your own opinion'*. What is more important is to remain flexible and to keep as many possibilities open as you can. For example, you should never use the word 'never'! Try to leave things as vague as you can at the end of any discussion. The priority is not to win the battle but to keep the relationship going.

Don't be afraid to lose an argument

Sometimes couples go on arguing until one wins or proves their point. The fact that they are in a competition means that neither of them can give in without losing face. However, if one partner deliberately decides to give in, and makes it clear that they are doing so, the other partner is faced with a dilemma. He/she can either go on with the argument and insist on winning, probably eventually feeling guilty for having done so, or both partners can join together and work cooperatively. It is often better for both to find a way of getting out of the argument.

Try not to blame the other person

This is of course easier said than done, but it is still worth the effort. Very few things in life are one person's fault exclusively. In relationships there is always a long series of interactions leading up to a crisis, and each partner has to a greater or lesser extent contributed to the situation (see under systemic theories in Chapter 2). One possible way of dealing with the problem is to outlaw all discussion of blame and to proceed with the discussion as far as possible without criticising.

Try to keep the discussion focused on the present and future

A good and constructive discussion will usually avoid too many recriminations, and a good way to avoid these is to focus mainly on what you are doing in the 'here and now' or on your plans for the immediate future. It is easier to avoid blame if you can keep away from the past in your discussions. If you are able to do so, concentrate on planning what you can do about the problems rather than trying to establish the causes of them.

Exercise: Communication Training

- Set up the timed discussion as in the exercise on page 120–121 (ten minutes without interruption).
- Decide what you want to talk about (it might be a recent TV programme, a book or a magazine article that one or both of you has read).
- Speak from the 'I' position; in other words start your sentences with 'I'.
- Speak in short sentences and leave a gap for your partner to respond.
- Show that you understand where your partner is coming from (empathise).
- Respect your partner's sensitivities.
- Try to end everything you say with a positive comment.
- Keep to the topic under discussion.
- Try not to blame each other.
- Avoid making summing up or closing remarks; leave issues open.
- Don't be afraid to lose an argument even if you still disagree.
- If your views are at odds with your partner's, 'agree to differ'.

Negotiation

Good communication is only half the battle when it comes to solving your relationship problems. The other half is negotiation, and this is the technique which seems to be getting the best results in research work on couple therapy. It is important always, as above, to be specific, keep to the point, remain flexible, don't mind-read and don't blame. There are, however, several other things to remember when it comes to negotiating, and the next section will deal with some of these.

Convert your complaints into requests

As with the process of communication, the first principle of negotiation is to work on the future rather than the past. All complaints are by definition placed in the past, and the first thing to do is to change that by converting them into requests or wishes. For example, if a woman says to her partner *'I hate you coming in so late from work'*, this could be put the other way around as *'I would like you to be home earlier from work'*. It should be clear to you that the second, positive, future form of words is much more likely to get a positive response from her partner than the first one. Almost all complaints can be reworded in this way, giving the partner the possibility of complying with the request.

Make the requests more specific

The next skill that is necessary in trying to negotiate is to make the request more specific. For example, if you say to your partner *'I would like you to be more positive towards me'*, that is a bit difficult for him/her to interpret. It isn't clear where, when or how you want that more positive response. It has to be more specific. For example, if you say *'I would be much happier if you would back me up when we are in George's company'*, this is more something that your partner can clearly understand, relate to and do for you.

Your request may be a lot more practical than that. It may be that you want to say *'I want you to be more helpful around the house'*. Again this is too general, and it would be better to say *'I would really like you to help with the vacuuming'*. The more specific a request is, the easier it is to understand and to act on.

The emphasis must be on the future

The previous two examples are both quite good from this angle. They are both 'future orientated', and can therefore form part of a negotiation. Talking about what happened in the past, even if it is true and relevant, is likely to get a defensive response. A request for future help or support is more easily responded to and more easily monitored by you.

The requests should be translated into tasks

The question of doing the vacuuming and supporting you in front of George are still requests, and now need to be put in the form of tasks. Ideally these should specify when, where and how they should be carried out. You may have a weekly routine of house tidying, and the vacuuming could be slotted into this at a time which is convenient to both partners. Similarly the meetings with George probably happen at predictable times, and the tasks can be limited to those times. You may even want to specify the issues you want support on, such as when, for example, George ridicules your political beliefs or your taste in music.

The tasks should be reciprocal, so that each partner has something they can do for the other

This is one of the most important aspects of negotiation. The partners should feel at the end of a negotiation session that they have both had their say in making requests and in setting tasks. Ideally there should be one, or at the most two, tasks for each partner in play at any one time, and the number of tasks should be equal between them. Thus the woman may request that the man looks after their baby while she goes out with her friends, while the man may request that the woman in turn lets him go out to the pub with his friends. If this sort of bargain is struck, the number of times per week that each task is to be carried out should be specified, and ideally this should be about equal for both partners.

It is not easy to achieve this kind of agreement the first time that you try, and there may be a fair number of trials before you get it right. However, it is usually well worth trying something like this in order to get away from the repetitive struggles that people get into.

Making sure that the tasks are practicable

Before settling on the tasks to be done by both partners, it is important to make sure that both of you agree that they are practicable and fair. This will require all your negotiating skills, and it is not always possible to get it right the first time. It may require you both to make compromises, for example to settle on fewer nights going out than you would ideally like, or making a different division of household chores. The key is to be practicable, and that may mean one partner at first making a few concessions in order to get the process going.

It is also a good idea to set tasks which are within the daily life that you have as a couple. There is little point in setting up plans to have an expensive holiday or an extension on the house as part of your exchange of positive behaviour. It is much safer to settle on things such as weeding the garden, looking after children or doing the weekly shopping, since these can be repeated on a weekly or daily basis and you can meet frequently to discuss progress on them.

Having a meeting to assess whether the tasks have been done

After a certain time (maybe a week) it is useful to have a meeting to check whether both partners have been carrying out their side of the reciprocal arrangements. This should ideally be part of the regular communication meetings, maybe on a weekly basis. It is not a disaster if (as usually happens) all the tasks have not been completed. What we are looking for is an improvement on the previous situation, and some indication that the relationship has improved in terms of mutual satisfaction.

Revising the mutual tasks at the weekly meetings

It is almost certainly going to be necessary to revise the reciprocal tasks at this weekly meeting, and if it has been impracticable to do some of them it may be necessary to make the difficult ones easier. Again, you may have to make a slightly uneven division in order to keep the process going forward. If there has been a very uneven division of labour for months or years, it may be difficult to change this over-night, and the best you can hope for at this stage is to get something reciprocal in place without worrying whether it is completely fair. The new arrangement is, in any case, likely to be an improvement on what went before, as at least the new arrangements are based on some discussion rather than just having arisen by long-standing habit.

CASE EXAMPLE

Richard (39) and Marion (41) have a five-year-old daughter, Amy, who is quite lively. They are both sports professionals, and Richard has a very busy schedule, while Marion works only part-time. They have a troubled marriage, in which Marion complains about Richard's time away from home, and his habit of bringing unexpected guests home late in the evening. He complains that she keeps nagging him about looking after Amy, reminding him that Amy needs her teeth-cleaning to be checked and her clothes ready to go to school. They also have a rather inactive sex life, which upsets Richard.

In negotiation they agreed that he was capable of looking after Amy without constant reminders, and that she would stop these. He also agreed to let her know about any plans for visitors before the visit happened, and said that he would restrict the frequency of these.

Their communication was sometimes very bitter, for example when he said 'I don't love you, I don't even like you', and she said 'You don't care for Amy and me, you just go off and do your own thing'. They managed to moderate the words in these communications, and became more polite and friendly in their dealings.

The sexual relationship remained rather inactive, because Richard was sensitive to rejection and cautious over initiating, while Marion found it almost impossible to make the first move. They agreed that they would try to get to bed at the same time, and that she would 'roll over' to his side so that if he wanted to initiate she would be available and would give him a more positive response. Their sex life increased considerably after this.

This case example shows how negotiation, communication training and the change in bedtime routines improved the couple's sexual and general relationship.

Be realistic about possible changes

This technique is not going to change the whole relationship immediately, but it is likely to make some worthwhile improvements, and it is always better to take note of the small improvements that have taken place rather than concentrate on all the remaining difficulties. Improvements are built on small steps, and you need to appreciate the small changes that your partner may have made if there is to be a chance that you will both be able to get out of the vicious circle of complaints that began the problems.

Try to think positively

It is very easy to get into negative and generalised patterns of thought (see Chapter 2), for example assuming that one setback in the process of self-help means that the whole thing has been a waste of time, and there is no hope for the relationship. Try to avoid this kind of negative thinking. It may be helpful to write down some of the minor improvements that have been achieved, in order to get away from these negative patterns of thinking and to concentrate on the achievements that have been made.

Exercise: Negotiation

- Set up the timed discussion with no distractions, as in the talk exercise on pages 120–121 (ten minutes to begin with).
- You need to communicate well, as in the communication exercise on page 132.

- Each partner should come with one specific complaint.
- The complaint should be about everyday life together.
- Partner A states their complaint in the form of a positive wish (for the immediate future).
- The wish is translated into a task for Partner B to carry out (specifying where, when, how and how often to do it).
- The task is set up, preferably in writing, by you both.
- You do the same with Partner B's complaint, converting it into a wish and then a task for partner A.
- You end the session with one written task each.
- At the next session (next week, next day or anything in between) you monitor how the tasks have gone.
- Don't expect both to achieve equal success, just note whether things are in any way improved from the previous situation.
- Don't rest on your laurels; you will need to continue with the process for a number of weeks, and you won't achieve a complete 'cure', but rather a changed way of treating each other for the future.

Working alone on improving the relationship

This brings us to the second part of this chapter, in which we try to help you to work on your relationship even if you cannot persuade your partner to cooperate. There may be all sorts of reasons why this is happening, but the most common might be that your uncooperative partner feels that there is not really a problem, and puts your discontent down to overreaction or neurosis. In this case there is still a lot to be said for trying to improve the relationship, and this can to some extent be done by one partner acting alone.

Become a good behaviourally orientated therapist

The methods used by behavioural psychologists (see Chapter 2, page 31), based on the work of B. F. Skinner, are well tried in all sorts of situations, and can be applied to a partner in a relationship very effectively. Some of you may have seen the series *Little Angels* on BBC television. Here the psychologists and psychotherapists use behavioural principles to help parents to control the behaviour of very unruly and disruptive young children. The ideas are the same as the ones outlined in Chapter 2, see pages 34–35, namely that if you reward behaviour (in this case good behaviour) it is more likely to be repeated. The most important message from this body of work is that if you want someone to do something, the best way is to reward him/her after they have done it. This makes them feel more positive about doing it again and makes it more likely that they will repeat the behaviour. These methods are just as effective with adults.

Rewarding 'good' behaviour

Reward, sometimes called positive reinforcement, is the most reliable way of getting someone to change their behaviour (see Chapter 2). Supposing your partner is always coming in late from work, and you have become rather irritated about it, you have probably tried complaining without making any difference to the behaviour. A more effective way to alter the lateness might be to notice when he/she comes in a bit earlier and say how pleased you are about it. If you can be consistent about this praise, if you can produce some other reward such as a hug or a treat, and if you can in addition be particularly friendly and positive towards your partner on those nights, the message will get across. If your partner is very late, however, you should be rather distant and quiet, taking little notice of them for a period of time (perhaps about five minutes) before you revert to your usual behaviour. If you then monitor the nightly time of arrival, you should find that there is a reduction in the lateness.

Dealing with 'bad' behaviour: ignore, don't complain

The paradoxical thing is that complaining about something like lateness is likely to act as a reward, which may increase the behaviour: your partner is given attention (which might take the form of a complaint) on arrival, and there is no special privilege resulting from being on time. If, however, you can ignore your partner for a while after they arrive late, this is a form of extinction (see page 35), which is likely to result in a reduction of the behaviour, especially if associated with special attention (see the previous paragraph) if the person is punctual. This is something that you will have to work on by trial and error, and it may not be clear at first that it is having any effect. However, if you make a chart of how late your partner is day by day it may then become clear that you are making progress.

How can you improve communication if you are working alone?

This too is a tall order, but if you try to be a good communicator (see above) you will probably find that your partner changes his/her style of communication in return. He/she will find it difficult to oppose you, to have an argument or to cause tension, if you make the decision to respond in a new and different way, for example by agreeing with him/her. What it takes more than anything is for you to show consistency, and if you can persevere in using all the skills we have described in the first part of this chapter, you will find that, even if you are working alone to improve the situation, your relationship can't be quite the same as it was before.

Should you tell your partner what you are doing?

Usually it is best to be open with your partner even if they are uncooperative, and if you explain the way you are trying to work, it may be that you will persuade them to work with you. However, it is still possible to manage changes in communication without their cooperation, and the bottom line is that if you want to change things badly enough you will be able to do it.

Can you manage to negotiate with your partner without their cooperation?

Again this is a difficult one, but you have to see the negotiation as a way of altering the way that the two of you interact. If you are consistent in keeping to your plans, you may be able to see a difference in the relationship as your partner realises that the new arrangements have some benefit for them also. For example, if your partner complains that you never clear up your papers, you could say that you will clear them up conscientiously if he/she agrees to tidy the bedroom. You continue to clear up your papers, and if there is any improvement in the state of the bedroom, however slight, you praise him/her for it. The relationship is likely to be less tense because of the increase in effective cooperation, even though your partner may say that he/she hasn't changed. Also, your morale will be improved because you are doing something active to improve the relationship, rather than just accepting that there is nothing you can do. If small changes are noticed you will feel that there has been some justification for the work.

(NOTE: The next two sections are relevant whether you are working together or unilaterally.)

Helping the improvements to last

When you have made some worthwhile improvements in your relationship, it is tempting to rest on your laurels and assume that it will now be all right, or to think that love has come back and that there is no need to worry any more. However much things have improved, you are both still the same people, with the same basic ways of relating, and things could easily go wrong again if you are not vigilant.

Have regular meetings even if things are going well

These should take a similar form to the meetings you had earlier, with both of you coming with an agenda and dividing the time between you. You might also use the timer that you used before, depending on whether you think you still need a limit to the time for discussion.

Think about what you yourself have done to change things

One of the hardest things for partners to do in this situation is to recognise what they themselves have done to improve the relationship. It is much easier to point out how your partner has changed. If a change has happened, look at the way you yourself might have contributed to that change. But the ultimate take-home message is that, whatever you have done to improve the situation, you should continue doing it, as indeed your partner should continue doing whatever they have been doing to improve things.

What would you both have to do wrong to bring the problems back?

This is another way of saying the same thing. But it puts it even more pointedly, because it emphasises that you have indeed done something positive yourself to improve things, and that you have the power to change them for better or for worse. If you think about this, it puts you in a position of both power and responsibility. It means that you accept that you may have contributed to the previous problems, and also to the improvements, and that you are not necessarily just the victim of your partner's whims and unpredictable behaviour.

If it goes really badly wrong, go back to square one

Things may, of course, go wrong even after a successful use of the techniques outlined here, but this is not the end of the world, or even the end of the story. You might decide to go back to the beginning of the chapter, try the exercises of communication and negotiation as before, and, with the knowledge of how they went wrong, you may be able to learn from your experience and be more successful. The key thing to remember is to persevere with the altered behaviour on a daily basis.

As we mentioned in Chapter 1, there is one basic rule for sustaining a long-term relationship, and that is to maintain toleration and patience, and to give your partner the benefit of the doubt. If you can commit yourselves to that rule, the rest will come more easily, both in the short term, while you are working on the problem, and in the longer term when both of you may forget the techniques you have been using.

If there is no improvement using these ideas and techniques

There are two options open to you in this event. Either you can move to Chapter 6, which takes a broader look at the problems and gives more wide-ranging suggestions as to solving them using a 'systemic' approach; or alternatively you may decide that the 'do-it-yourself' way is not going to be successful, and seek professional help from a counsellor or therapist (see the list in Useful addresses, page 339).

Key Points

- The only person you can really change is your-self, and by changing your own behaviour you will be able to alter your partner's behaviour.
- It is very important, though often difficult, to talk together if you have problems.
- The safest way to do this is to call a truce and set up ten-minute discussion sessions.
- You should prepare a script with one or two points each to talk about.
- You should divide the time equally between you.

- If arguments happen you could either try to let them run on and end by 'agreeing to differ' or alternatively stop the session and plan another one in a day or two.
- The principles of good communication are to be brief, positive, specific, show empathy and be sensitive to your partner's feelings.
- These principles can be included in your timed talk sessions.
- Negotiation depends on converting complaints to wishes, and wishes to tasks. The tasks should be practicable and roughly equal between you, and they may be monitored week by week.
- If you are working as an individual to improve your relationship problems, you should become a good behaviourally orientated therapist and reward the behaviour you want to encourage, while ignoring whatever you want your partner to stop doing.
- These methods do not provide a cure for your problems, but should give you a new way of controlling them.

6

Self-help: timetables, arguments, triangles and maintaining the boundaries

If communicating and negotiating are now all right but you still have a problem

Supposing you have gone through all the exercises in the previous chapter, but still have a problem with the relationship. It may not be enough to communicate and negotiate well; you may need to look at other aspects of the relationship, including the boundaries between you and the boundaries around you as a couple. In this chapter our plan is to look at other ways of helping couples with problems when the simpler approaches do not seem to work. We will be covering this in four stages:

- First is the question of how to define whose problem it is;

- next we will suggest some more creative techniques to help with the difficulties;
- then we will be dealing with some outside factors (including other people and work pressures) which may be contributing to the problems;
- and finally we will be suggesting some 'last ditch' solutions which might be preferable to splitting up.

Whose problem is it?

How to avoid unnecessary labelling

One reason why communicating and negotiating might not work is that you may have located the problem in one partner rather than in the relationship. It's often an arbitrary choice whether to think of the issue as consisting of one partner's 'bad behaviour' or 'personality problem' or whether to put the blame on a relationship difficulty between the partners. The advantage of thinking of it as a couple relationship problem is that it becomes possible for both partners to change their behaviour in a minor way, rather than one partner changing more radically. Sometimes of course there is a real personality problem on one partner's side, and in Chapter 8 we will be describing some of the ways that genuine psychological and psychiatric problems affect the couple. However, wherever possible, it is better in our view to deal with most of these 'individual' problems by modifying the relationship. Some of the patterns which may wrongly lead to the labelling of one partner as ill or disturbed are outlined in this section.

Exclusivity versus openness

In this type of relationship the more open partner might label the more secretive one as being pathologically shy or even paranoid, while the more secretive one might say the other is flirtatious or a gossip. Neither description is very helpful, because the assumption is that the partner who applies the label is completely 'normal' and has no need to change, whereas the labelled partner must mend their ways. A better solution is for the couple to discuss how to achieve a compromise position on the question of openness, which may not be ideal for either of them, but which may be tolerated by both.

Pessimism versus optimism

This is another difference that may be escalated into a label of abnormal behaviour. The pessimistic partner may feel that the optimistic one is irresponsible and far too trusting of people and systems. The optimist may feel that the pessimist is depressed or pathologically anxious, and dismiss their concerns as neurotic. Actually, they both have valid points of view, in that one is seeing life as a glass that is half empty while the other perceives it as a glass that is half full.

The couple should try to reach a compromise, looking at those issues which they disagree about and either dividing the responsibilities between them or deciding on a jointly agreed course of action which does not offend either partner.

Control versus laissez-faire (see Chapter 4 under 'You're bossy!', page 97)

Some couples have a difference over how much they should be involved with each other's life, decision making and activities. The more controlling partner may again feel that the more easygoing one is irresponsible and needs to be helped to make sensible decisions, while the more easy-going one may resent the intrusiveness of the controlling partner. It could be seen as the controlling partner trespassing over the other one's personal boundary. This issue is perhaps more difficult for the couple to work out than the preceding ones. However, it should be possible to reach a compromise, which may have to be a different one for each specific situation that demands decisions to be made.

CASE EXAMPLE

Arthur (45) and Mary (46) had been married for twenty-nine years. They had a son and daughter, aged 27 and 21. Arthur had been wrongly labelled by both himself and Mary as 'depressed' for the previous twenty years, and Mary had spent much time and effort trying to get the best treatment for him. The couple came for therapy because they wanted to have a fresh look at the problem. Arthur asked Mary to describe his problems, because he said she would give a more accurate account of it than he could. The behaviour she described consisted mainly of tantrums when he was intoxicated, and there was only a small part of the problem which was typical of depression. It seemed that the couple had effectively labelled their power struggles and communication problems as being due to Arthur's 'depression'. In therapy they were able to get away from Mary's tendency to treat him as an irresponsible child, and in the process he began taking more responsibility for his own actions and decisions. Having been unemployed, he found a good job, and felt much more relaxed about life. Mary, however, went through a period of considerable stress while getting used to Arthur's new independence, and had to be supported while she reduced her own employment pressures by taking part-time work. In fact, Arthur turned out to be quite a good 'nurse' for her when she had to rest because of her 'fatigue and malaise'. This is a good example of the inappropriate labelling of Arthur's 'depression', and the way that the partners with the 'control versus laissez-faire' problem were able to resolve their differences.

The case of Arthur and Mary illustrates what is quite a common problem: the controlling partner enrols the medical services to treat the other one for what eventually turns out to be a relationship problem. Even when the problem is legitimately medical, as in some cases of depression or morbid jealousy (Chapter 8) there are still things that the couple can do to alleviate the stresses on them.

Closeness and distance

Intimacy may be sexual, emotional, physical or operational (see Chapter 2, page 46–47). For some people the sexual side is the only kind of intimacy that is important to them, and this is fine as long as it suits both partners. However, when a couple is made up of two individuals with different intimacy needs, problems may arise.

Different needs for sexual and emotional intimacy

If, for example, you value emotional sharing and your partner only wants you for sex, there may be a mismatch which threatens the continuation of the relationship. One possible solution is a timetable (see below) in which you agree to be intimate emotionally at certain agreed times during the week and sexually at other times. Another way to cope with this problem is for the person with the need for emotional intimacy to meet with a friend or relative with whom they can satisfy their need for emotional sharing and treat the partner as someone to be on friendly and sexual, but not emotionally intimate, terms with.

Emotional and physical closeness

There is another form of closeness which is physical without being sexual. This is characterised by the way that couples who are quite intimate tend, for instance, to straighten each other's clothing or pick fluff off a jacket. It is a pleasant form of closeness, and shows care for each other, although it can also have an implication of possessiveness, which may not be totally welcome to one of the two. Again some people may feel that the physical closeness is not enough and they need some extra sharing of feelings as well. It is often the man who is less comfortable with emotional closeness, and the woman who wants to be closer. As with the sexual/emotional problem, an agreement to be emotionally close at planned, but limited, times in the day may begin to help (see 'timetables' below).

Operational closeness

In general, each person has his/her preference as to how close or distant they should be in a relationship. This type of closeness, which we can call operational closeness, is mainly concerned with how much time the couple spend together, and whether they live together or apart. It is also relevant to the question of how much they share plans and how much they know about each other's daily activities. Much of the implicit negotiation that goes on when a relationship is forming is to do with the question of operational closeness. One partner may feel very strongly that they want to be part of a closely knit and exclusive couple, while the other wants to have a bit more freedom of movement. The methods outlined in Chapter 5 suggest how to negotiate these issues in a peaceful and constructive way.

Does one of you want to do things that the other one hates? Timetables may help

There are many examples of this type of problem within any relationship. We are referring to those activities that one partner really needs to do and the other finds boring or off-putting. Here are some examples:

- Wanting to talk (even to argue) late into the night
- Watching sports programmes on television
- Watching the news on television
- Watching soap operas on television
- Vacuum cleaning late at night (could interfere with sex!)
- Wanting to interrogate the partner (jealousy)
- Wanting more sex than the partner does
- Wanting to go shopping together
- Sitting at the computer
- Visits to relatives
- Attendance at sports clubs

The list could be extended, but such disputes are very common and can often be troublesome. How could you resolve them?

Suppose that you have a dispute about what to watch together on TV (for example sports or soap operas). If

Partner A wants to do a lot of this and Partner B wants to watch other things, or simply to talk more, you could work out a timetable in which each 'activity' is rationed to certain hours each day. Similarly, timetables could be set up for when one partner might be sitting at the computer (a common problem in these days of easy internet access) or for doing housework such as vacuum cleaning at unpopular times (e.g. late at night). In all cases it would be helpful for Partner B (who is bored or put off by the activity) to offer to do something instead which is popular with Partner A, and which may be seen as a reward for reducing the activity.

The value of timetables

Wherever there is something in their relationship that a couple, or even one partner, feels to be out of control, there is a chance that a timetable will help to solve the problem. It is not necessarily the whole answer, and it may not have to be used for long before things settle down and the timetable can be discontinued. What the timetable essentially does is to treat both partners' needs as legitimate, and simply to say that there should be a fair division of their lives together into time that is rewarding for Partner A and time that is rewarding for Partner B.

Timetables may therefore be seen as a fair way of re-arranging a couple's time together, and making it rewarding for the partner who is giving something up by providing an alternative way of spending the time. They may also be used in more serious conflict situations, such as a partner who is excessively jealous (see Chapter 8), a partner who desires sex more frequently than the other partner (see Chapter 7) or a couple who are having intractable arguments and fights (see Chapter 9).

Exercise: Setting a Timetable

- You need to establish what the activities are that need to be timetabled.
- Get together, if necessary using a time-limited discussion (see Chapter 5) with no distractions such as TV, music or radio, and the telephone on 'silent'.
- The partner who is feeling uncomfortable about the activity should say what the problem is and what they would like to be done.
- The other partner should then make an offer for a timetable.
- You should then agree on how long the activity should go on for, and how often.
- Then you need to plan for the time when it should happen, how long for and how often (for example a visit to Partner A's relatives on a weekend once a month for four hours).
- For some activities there should be more specification (for example Partner A to sit at the computer for a maximum of three hours on Monday, Wednesday and Friday).

- You might like to think of a mutual timetable, for example watching sports on TV for two hours twice a week and soap operas for half an hour daily.

How to increase mutual understanding (empathy)

You may feel that you are fairly good at communicating, but that there is something missing in your emotional rapport, or empathy, and that this is getting in the way of being open with each other.

Beware of too much openness (see Chapter 5)

Before getting into the ways in which you can achieve more openness, a word of caution. In even the closest relationships there are some things that you might be wise to keep to yourself. A man who walks along the road with his wife and says *'Look at that attractive girl over there'*, is playing with fire if his wife is worried about her own attractiveness. Similarly, a woman who praises a friend's ability to understand her may be taking a risk if her partner feels that by implication she is saying that he doesn't understand her.

Try 'reversed role-play'

If you have real difficulty getting into your partner's mind, it may be worth trying a technique called 'reversed role-play'.

Exercise: Reversed Role-play

- Sit down together with no distractions (TV, music, telephone or radio) and the timer set for ten minutes.
- If you are used to sitting in your favourite place or chair, change places.
- Start to have a discussion, perhaps about some fairly ordinary subject that you disagree on (but not something serious like religion or education) but take your partner's point of view.
- Perhaps you might change your voice tone and use the kinds of reasoning that your partner usually uses.
- Try to enter into your partner's way of thinking about the subject.
- This means, of course, arguing the opposite case from the one you would normally support.
- At the end, perhaps for the next ten minutes, you should change back to your usual chair, your own voice and your own point of view.
- Try to talk together about the discussion you had, and discuss how it felt to be taking your partner's side, and exploring their way of thinking.

This exercise is an interesting one that we have tried many times in the couple therapy clinic, and it usually helps the partners to gain a greater degree of empathy with each other.

How to argue safely

This is in some ways an easier exercise, in that you just have to argue from your own point of view. However, it is also a bit more risky, in that the argument could get out of hand, and if you are in the habit of having fierce arguments already, with the risk of violence, this exercise may not be for you (see Chapter 9).

Arguments can be healthy for the couple

Every couple from time to time argues, and for most it is a necessary way to express their differences and hopefully resolve them. Thus arguments are not a disaster to be avoided, but a healthy way of interacting which can make the relationship interesting and lively. Problems arise because sometimes you say things which cannot be taken back, and this may sour the relationship to the extent that you might even think of separation. Even when arguments don't reach this level of destructiveness, there is always the risk that things may get out of hand, and for this reason many couples try to avoid them altogether.

Deciding to have an argument

In our therapeutic work we have found that in many

couples, especially those who have a very bland and polite relationship, a healthy argument can clear the air, and we actually encourage couples to have arguments in the session in the presence of the therapist. They are asked to choose trivial topics to argue about.

Choose a trivial topic

If you decide to try this approach, you should find something that you disagree about, but which is not too serious, and which you can allow to rumble on without real harm coming to the relationship. An example might be the toothpaste tube. Almost all couples have their differences about this, one partner preferring to squeeze it from the bottom, and the other either not minding or preferring to squeeze it from the middle. Another one might be what to do about dirty clothes. One partner might prefer them to be put in a laundry basket or a special place in the bathroom, while the other may feel that the bedroom floor is the best place until something can be done about washing them. These two topics are both essentially trivial (although we realise that for some people these areas are more important than they might be for others) and they are usually capable of bearing two different points of view.

Plan a limited time for the argument

As previously suggested (see Chapter 5), if you are planning an exercise, whether it is an exercise in communication, negotiation or arguing, it is safest to allow only a limited time for it, such as ten minutes at first, and to make sure that you have a way of separating from each other at the end. The best way to ensure this is to set a timer at the beginning and to stop the exercise and move into separate rooms at the end. You should ideally not raise the topic again until the next planned exercise in arguing.

How to structure the time

The argument should be good-natured and humorous if possible, and the topic should be trivial enough for it not to matter if you can't agree at the end. In fact, it is probably better for you not to reach an agreement, but to shelve the issue or 'agree to differ' as you finish the session. It could then be possible to have the same argument on a future occasion, with the same opinions being expressed by you both and the same lack of a conclusion at the end. The important thing about these exercises is the process of arguing and expressing your opinions openly and forcefully; the conclusion you reach is unimportant. The only vital issue is that you respect your partner's right to have a different opinion from yours.

Who would be helped by arguments?

This approach is not really necessary for all couples. It is best used by those couples who have had difficulty in expressing emotions or who 'never have an angry word'. Most couples have areas which they cannot agree on, and there is no shame in that. The problem is that sometimes the fact that you never discuss your unresolved differences can sour an otherwise good relationship.

Exercise: Trivial Arguments

- Sit down together with no distractions (TV, music, telephone or radio) and set the timer for ten minutes.
- Choose a trivial topic that you have differing views on (toothpaste tubes or dirty clothes are good examples).
- Argue the case in a light-hearted manner.
- Don't let it get too serious.
- Keep to the topic, don't get into other controversial areas.
- Don't start name-calling or insulting each other.
- When the timer goes, stop and go to separate rooms.
- Respect each other's point of view without agreeing to it.
- It's OK to talk about it afterwards, but stick mainly to discussing how it felt to be arguing, and don't resurrect the argument until the next planned session.

(For a case example of an argument see Chapter 7, page 218.)

Triangles and boundary issues

In this section we will be describing the way in which the couple can be affected by outside factors, which might consist of work pressures, children, relatives or friends. In many cases these situations could be described as taking the form of triangles, in which the partners, whose relationship might be seen as a straight line between two points, are reacting as a team in relation to a third person or thing (the point of the triangle). The 'point' of the triangle also has the power to draw one partner away from the relationship into a new alliance with the outside individual.

Triangles of course are almost universal in human experience. Mostly they cause no difficulty, and they may be a positive thing and a source of pleasure. In this part of the chapter, however, we will be mainly dealing with the problems that might be caused by triangular situations. The common problem of the triangle created by the birth of a baby we have already mentioned in Chapter 4, page 108. Other types of triangle will be outlined here, with possible ways of dealing with them.

The triangular situation, whether involving people or things, could also be thought of as raising the issue of the boundaries around the couple, in which they have to decide how much they are working as a team and how much they are two separate individuals. Because of the profound effect that these situations can have on the couple, you need to be as clear as you can about where your boundaries are and how tight they are.

Triangles involving children

Some of the most common triangular situations involve your children. Children can show their distress in many ways, from overactive behaviour in a young child to teenage rebellion or anorexia in an older one, or severe arguments and fights between siblings. It may be that the child's behaviour problem is partly caused by tensions between the parents. The behaviour of the child may be seen as a cry for help, not only for the child but also for the whole family. The child whose parents are at loggerheads is going to feel insecure, and will often behave badly as an expression of that insecurity. The behaviour can have two positive results for the child: firstly it may bring the parents closer together, and secondly it may give the child a greater sense of power within the family. These results are, however, bought at a price, in that the child will feel more insecure than before, and sometimes this insecurity (which is connected with a fear that his/her parents are too weak to be in control) will lead to an escalation of the behaviour. A vicious circle then builds up, with more parental anxiety leading to more of the problem behaviour, leading to recriminations between the parents, and this in turn leading to a greater sense of insecurity on the part of the child.

What is the answer?

There is a set of techniques based on behavioural principles which has been very successful in helping parents to cope with badly behaved children (see the section on behavioural principles in Chapter 2, page 34-35). The two main principles are to reward desired behaviour and to ignore undesired behaviour. Punishment, on the other hand, can disrupt behaviour in the short term, but has unpredictable results, and is usually ineffective in the longer run. In order for the behavioural rewards to work, you must work as a team, and in some ways this teamwork may be as important as the techniques themselves. A case, which is based on several different families, may make this clearer.

CASE EXAMPLE

David, aged 6, is a lively and intelligent boy, who is quite jealous of the attention his mother (Jennie, 25) gives to his younger brother Mark (3). His father, John (26), is out much of the time, and Jennie is the main carer for the boys. On shopping trips, David continually embarrasses Jennie by having tantrums, especially when she does not give him the sweets or toys he wants. In therapy Jennie would be encouraged to give David a lot of attention when he is being 'good', with a constant programme of keeping him interested and amused, for example by making a game out of his helping her with the shopping. If, however, he has a tantrum, she would be encouraged to ignore him, however embarrassing it is, perhaps explaining to critical bystanders that this is an important part of his learning experience. This way, he realises that there is no reward for tantrums, and will soon begin to cooperate with Jennie. It would be even more effective if John can go with them on some of the shopping trips and if both parents share in the management of the two boys. John should also back Jennie up in keeping David interested in the shopping or other activity while ignoring the tantrums. The prediction is that David will also feel more secure in the new family atmosphere, in which he is a valued collaborator rather than an uncontrolled rebel.

Many people do not realise that their children need quite a lot of attention when they are with their parents, and will work to get it, for example by misbehaving, by teasing their siblings or by being destructive. Parents who only give their children attention when they are naughty, even if that attention is in the form of telling them off or punishing them, are actually encouraging naughty behaviour. The alternative way outlined above (ignoring the bad behaviour) is a better way. It is labour-intensive at first, especially in the planning of activities which interest the problem child, while at the same time not neglecting the younger brother. However, in the end it saves time and effort, and can help to avoid the progressive alienation of the problem child.

What about other forms of childhood behaviour problems?

Sometimes a child will seem to monopolise one parent, sharing secrets with that parent and making them promise not to tell the other one what is being discussed. This is a classic example of the parent being 'triangulated' by the child, away from their partner. In this case it is important for the parents to be a parental team, and to act together in the care of the children. So, when a child makes a request of one parent to keep something secret from the other, it would be better not to promise to keep the secret, but to say that the parents don't have secrets from each other. We will return to this topic in Chapter 11, in connection with blended families, where the child–parent relationships, especially in a recently formed family, are much more problematic.

Triangles involving family of origin

Both partners in a relationship are usually in touch with their own parents, and although this is usually a great support for them, it can sometimes cause difficulties. The problem may arise where, say, the parents of Partner A do not approve of their son/daughter's partner, and conflict arises. The dilemma for Partner A is to keep both relationships going without losing either his/her parents or his/her partner. It may take quite a lot of skill to balance this situation and to keep the peace when the two antagonistic parties meet, for instance at Christmas and birthdays.

Another problem with families of origin is when Partner A's parents want to be a controlling influence in the relationship, especially where the rearing of children is involved. Their advice may be very good, but when Partner B (often the male in this situation) is bypassed in making important decisions about the children, for example about education or religion, he may feel neglected and resent it.

This situation may arise especially when children are very young, and their mother is insecure about parenting. The father may feel really out of touch, and either becomes a non-participant parent or fights for his parental influence, with negative consequences for the relationship. The answer, as is often the case, is for both partners to act as a team, to consult each other as much as possible and to discuss Partner A's mother's advice together before deciding whether to follow it.

CASE EXAMPLE

Liam (45) is married to Siobhan (42) and they have two boys, aged 10 and 8. Liam's mother, who has not worked outside the home, used to be very close to Siobhan, meeting her regularly to take the children out, and giving the children presents. There was a serious argument, however, between her and Siobhan, and Siobhan has now refused to see Liam's mother without Liam being present. The mother is very upset by this, and puts pressure on Liam to arrange meetings with Siobhan and the children. In therapy the couple agreed that it would be sensible for Liam to see his mother alone on a regular basis, and to arrange frequent family meetings including her, himself, his wife and children. The mother was not completely satisfied by this arrangement, but accepted it, and at their eldest son's first communion there was a pleasant family gathering with all attending. The important thing in this case is that the couple worked out their strategy (as the 'decider subsystem' – see Chapter 2) and then put it into practice with Liam's mother and the children.

Triangles involving friends, outside activities or work

Leisure activities

Often a couple find that they have very different interests, and that they don't really enjoy each other's activities. A young man may be very interested in sport, and have a commitment to a tennis club which is long-standing, and which involves quite a lot of socialising after matches. His new partner may find this very boring, and wishes that he would join her on shopping trips instead, an activity which he finds uninteresting. The two competing interests each form a kind of triangle for the relationship, and the problem may become so acute that it jeopardises the relationship. The answer is to discuss the competing interests as a couple, trying to find a compromise which suits both partners. This could take the form of a timetable (see above), in which both partners agree to give up some of their leisure activities for the sake of the relationship. If this cannot be done, and if both the activities annoy the opposite partner too much, they should perhaps think about the future of the relationship before they enter into too deep a commitment together.

Friends

Similar problems can arise with friends of both partners. If Partner A cannot get along with Partner B's friends, a decision may have to be made (as with the problem with parents mentioned above) as to which relationship Partner B is most committed to, and he/she will have to make arrangements to reduce the conflict, perhaps by meeting the friends without the partner or by dropping the friends for the partner's sake.

Work problems

Some jobs are very demanding, and one partner may be in such a job, with the need to work long hours or to spend time on long business trips, with no possibility of changing this without loss of earnings or damage to their career. However, the other partner may resent the time that their partner spends at work, and once again a triangle has formed which causes tension in the relationship. The person with the absorbing job may find it hard to understand why the other partner can't accept the importance of his/her career, while the other partner finds it hard to see why the demands of the job are given such high priority. Again the solution will depend on the importance each partner gives to the relationship and to the job. There isn't always an easy solution, but talking and trying to understand each other is the best that can be done.

What if all this doesn't work? The last resort

The 'housemates' solution

There may be couples who are unable to make use of the various ideas presented here, whether communication training, negotiation, timetables, arguments or sorting out triangles. What then if these techniques are all ultimately ineffective? Something we have found useful for couples who want to stay together, but are unable to change things so as to improve the relationship, is the idea of being 'good housemates' and (if there are children) co-parents, without trying to have a close marital relationship. There are some advantages to this arrangement compared with the otherwise inevitable separation or divorce. The advantage for the children is that they do not have to move or have alternating parental care, and they can retain their friends and outside interests. The couples who have adopted this policy have usually had children of school age, and the unspoken agreement is usually that they will eventually divorce, perhaps when the children have left school.

Lateral thinking and paradox

Sometimes in the face of insoluble relationship problems, it may be possible to adopt creative solutions which come from the couple's own ideas about the relationship. You may, for example, think of a completely crazy idea such as buying the house next door and living separately in both houses. You may divide up the family by sending the children to one or other set of grandparents, and you as a couple become weekend visitors. You may divide up the childcare differently, perhaps by the man becoming a house husband and the woman going out to work.

In some cases in our clinic, faced with the couple's inability to make any changes in their relationship, we have used the so-called paradox. In this we tell them that there is no real problem with the way that they are treating each other, however bad it seems to them, and however much they say they want to change it, because it has positive spin-offs for their relationship (such as creating excitement or providing stability). By thinking in this way the couple either feel a sense of relief that there is nothing that they can do about the problem, and relax and get on with their lives; or alternatively they tell the therapist they are wrong, and proceed to make the changes that then lead to improvement. This is, however, very much a last resort in terms of therapy, and we are careful not to use it indiscriminately.

Seeking professional help

There are now a large number of therapists and counsellors who are experienced in couple therapy (see Useful addresses, page 339), and if there is no improvement as a result of your own efforts, especially if this is due to your being unable to cooperate well enough to make progress with the techniques, you may wish to consider referring yourselves, or getting a referral (perhaps from your doctor) to a therapist or counsellor. The waiting list for relationship-counselling organisations is sometimes rather long, but there are private therapists/counsellors available, of whom we have given some details in the appendix.

Key Points

- It is often better to consider labelling a problem as being a relationship problem rather than one person's 'illness' because that way there is a greater possibility of solving it.
- When people differ in personality they may see the partner as being 'ill' when there isn't really anything wrong, just a clash of personalities.
- Couples can have problems with closeness and distance, and this may lead to conflict.
- If one partner needs to do something on a regular basis that the other partner dislikes, you may think of arranging a 'timetable' in which you agree to do it on a regular but controlled basis: this legitimises the activity without making it unbearable for the other partner.
- If you can't see your partner's point of view, you could try 'reversed role-play' in which you have a discussion taking each other's role (putting forward your partner's point of view).
- If you never argue, you might try exploring the process of arguing by having a trivial argument in

which you keep it light and humorous, but end by 'agreeing to differ'.

- Couples can be stressed by triangular situations, whether with children, parents, friends, work or leisure activities.
- Suggestions are made for how to deal with each of these stresses as a couple.
- If all else fails, you could decide to live as 'house-mates' for the sake of avoiding the trauma that divorce would cause for the children.

PART THREE

SPECIAL SITUATIONS

7

Coping with sexual problems

Problems of desire and problems of sexual function

We wrote in Chapter 3 about the differences between sexual drive, sexual desire, sexual arousal and orgasm. To recap:

- Sexual drive is a biologically determined need for sexual release, which is partly based on testosterone, especially in males, and there are differences between men and women in the way that sexual drive is expressed.

- Men seem to be more spontaneous and self-motivated in their sexual needs, and require a regular outlet (perhaps in self-stimulation) if they are not going to be frustrated; while women can enjoy sex just as much, and perhaps more, but can manage longer spells without it if they are not in a relationship.

- Sexual desire, on the other hand, is a desire for a particular sexual experience, maybe with a particular partner or maybe a specific kind of sexual activity, and sexual desire within a relationship is often the mainspring in its development and in its continuation.

- Sexual arousal is best described as biological readiness for a sexual experience. In the man this is usually shown by the presence of an erection, and in the woman by vaginal moistness or lubrication and clitoral enlargement. Desire and arousal usually happen at the same time, but in some cases of sexual dysfunction, this doesn't work: for example a man with erectile dysfunction may not have an erection even though his desire is strong, or a woman whose sexual desire is normal may be unable to be aroused because of anxiety.

- Orgasm is the climax of the sexual process, and involves a feeling of pleasure accompanied by ejaculation in the man, and a similar feeling of pleasure in the woman. This is usually followed by relaxation and satisfaction for both, but women can often move on to a second climax, while this is much rarer in men.

- Mutual orgasm, which some believe that all couples should experience, is not as common as is generally thought, and this is one area where unrealistic expectations can harm an otherwise good relationship.

Misunderstandings

Many people, both men and women, are shy or even embarrassed about discussing their sexual feelings, and often the problems of desire and sexual function get muddled up in discussion. It is helpful to be as plain as possible in discussing sex, but the most important thing is to respect your partner's sensitivities. Within these limits, a positive approach to talking about a sexual problem, being clear about what exactly is wrong, may do a lot of good and may make the problem much easier to cope with. This may be easy in couples who already have a sympathetic understanding of each other. However, there are some couples whose relationship flourishes on teasing and a combative approach to each other, and for them the move to being positive and sympathetic may be a more difficult one. Even if your relationship is of that sort, you may be able to have a constructive talk about sex if you follow the suggestions below.

How to start discussing sexual problems and difficulties

One of the hardest steps is to raise the subject for the first time. If a couple notice a sexual problem, it may be that the one with the problem feels embarrassed to talk about it, and may need some encouragement to do so. It may be easier for the other partner to raise it, but again this has to be done with care so as not to upset the partner with the problem. An exercise may help you to get into this area of discussion.

Talking about Your Sexual Problem

- Make sure that you are not going to be disturbed (turn off the radio, TV and music and put the telephone on 'silent').
- Sit comfortably together with the timer on (maybe for ten minutes at first).
- Come with an agenda for what you want to talk about.
- Start with a non-threatening issue such as arrangements for the evening or the time you go to bed.
- If it feels safe, go on to raise the sexual problem.
- Try and tune in to what the other person is wanting.
- If you have complaints, put them in the form of positive requests (see Chapter 5).
- Use all the communication and negotiation skills you have learned in Chapter 5.
- Use simple language that you both understand.
- Remember that non-sexual problems may be interfering with sex, and think about what you might be resentful about in your general relationship.
- Don't go on too long in discussion: if you have not reached a conclusion, put it 'on ice' until the next time.

Keeping your expectations realistic

Sex is usually better if you can get away from the media-inspired idea that every couple should have a satisfying sexual experience every day, with equal spontaneous levels of desire and simultaneous orgasms. Realistically, in most couples sex has to be fitted in with a busy career and/or family life, and is rarely ideal. The aim should be to set your own realistic goals and try to achieve them, bearing in mind that the best experiences will not happen very often.

We will now outline some of the ways that you may find helpful to start to deal with any problems or difficulties as they arise. Some of these will be very general and applicable in most circumstances whilst others are more specific for a particular problem or difficulty. Some of these may seem to be unnecessary on a first read but please bear with us and try some of these exercises at home. Above all else, try to approach these exercises with an open mind, showing curiosity about how it may be helpful, even in a small way, and above all, try to have fun during the sessions.

The exercise you could start with: relaxation and sensate focus

The pioneers of sexual therapy were Masters and Johnson in the USA. They were the first to treat the couple as the unit for therapy, and they concluded that in many people with sexual problems anxiety was a major factor. They even coined the term 'performance anxiety' to describe the anxiety that affects people with a sexual problem whenever they try to make love. In order to get over this performance anxiety they devised an exercise called sensate focus, in which the couple would have a kind of prolonged fore-play together with a ban on sexual intercourse. This tries to overcome the performance anxiety that they both feel when one of them has a problem, by reducing the fear of failure and helping 'physical communication', using touch rather than words to get across what each one needs or feels.

In our clinics we have found that it is useful to practise relaxation before doing the sensate focus exercise, so we will give you a guide to that technique at the beginning of this set of exercises.

Exercise: Relaxation and Non-sensate Genital Focus

In this exercise the idea is to get used to the feeling of physical closeness and 'physical communication' without the pressure of having to 'perform' sexually at the end. It involves relaxation and then a kind of prolonged foreplay without genital touching. There is a ban on intercourse and orgasm, at least for the first few times you do it. It is useful for any kind of sexual problem, whether in the man or the woman, and can lead on to more relaxed and satisfying sex.

- You will need at least forty-five minutes, so make sure that you choose a time when you have no interruptions or pressures on you (radio and TV off, and the telephone on 'silent').

- It is a good idea to prepare for the exercise by having a bath or shower, either separately or together.
- Make sure the room you are in is warm and comfortable, with a good bed or couch to lie on, and maybe some towels on the bed.
- It may help to have soft lights and some quiet music in the background, or you may prefer darkness and silence.
- You may also use body oil as a way of making the experience more sensuous, although some couples prefer talcum powder, and some prefer to use nothing.
- You should be careful to avoid touching any of the erogenous zones, including breasts, penis, testicles, vagina and clitoris, at least in the first few sessions.

The next step is to go to the bedroom together, lie down on the bed with no clothes on, but do feel able to use a cover (a towel or a sheet) at first if this will make relaxation easier and to practise relaxation. This is best done by relaxing your muscles accompanied by deep, slow breathing.

- Lie down on the bed, take a deep breath in, and tense your leg muscles.
- As you breathe out slowly, relax the leg muscles and keep them relaxed.

- Breathe in again and tense the muscles in your buttocks, and then relax them as you breathe out and keep them relaxed.
- Breathe in again and tense the muscles around the base of the penis and the muscles around the vagina, and then relax them as you breathe out (this is the Kegel exercise – see page 195).
- You then do the same with the muscles in your stomach (abdomen), relaxing them as you breathe out.
- Your chest muscles will naturally be tense as you breathe in, but as you breathe out you should try and leave them as relaxed as possible.
- You then tense your neck and shoulders, arms and hands, relaxing them as you breathe out.
- Finally, you make a face, clenching your jaw and screwing your eyes up, relaxing everything as you breathe out.
- At the end, breathe slowly and try to keep all those muscles as relaxed as possible.

This exercise underlines the way that, in order to get worked up sexually, it is often necessary to 'work down' first by relaxing.

You then take it in turns to stroke and caress each other, using the oil or the powder if you want, and only talking about what you are doing or experiencing (rather than general chat). It doesn't matter who starts, but for the sake of this description we will assume that it is the woman.

It is important to remember here that the same principles apply for couples in a same-sex relationship. We have not attempted to change the terminology from 'man' and 'woman' into 'partner 1' and 'partner 2' as this might be viewed as a very clinical and non-intimate way of describing the exercises that are meant to be undertaken in a light-hearted way and to be fun. We hope that this does not result in any feelings of disrespect from two men or two women readers who are in a same-sex relationship, as this is not our intention, and we hope that same-sex couples can use the exercises equally well.

- The man lies facedown, and the woman kneels and explores his body, beginning at the feet.
- Massage the toes, using the oil if you want, asking him how he likes you to do it, and going along with his wishes. Men often prefer a stronger touch, and women a lighter one, but the important thing is to do what your partner likes. Some men are ticklish, and the best way to overcome this is to use a heavier touch.
- Move on to the legs, then the backs of the upper legs, and then the buttocks. The woman as the active partner should try to enjoy the experience of caressing and touching, while the man should remain passive and receptive, enjoying what is happening, and only commenting if he would

like her to use a stronger or lighter touch, or describing his sensations and emotions.

- From the buttocks move on to the lower back, upper back and shoulders and then the neck, the arms and hands, and then massage the scalp, keeping the same touch as before.
- Then ask him to turn over, and stroke and caress him on his front, beginning from the feet and moving up the legs.
- Avoid the genital area at this stage, and move on to the stomach, chest, arms and hands.
- Stroke his face with your hands, and if you want to, kiss his face, eyes, ears and mouth (but passionate kissing may be a bit too strong at this stage).

Either of you may become sexually aroused during sensate focus, but you should still observe the ban on intercourse and orgasm. If a man has an erection this does not mean that he must immediately go on and have sex, either in intercourse or in masturbation. Just let the sensation stay or go away, and try not to let it get out of control. (The idea of the exercise is to get away from performance anxiety, and a rush to intercourse may cause the anxiety to rise. On the other hand, it would be all right for the man to ejaculate and for the woman to have an orgasm at the end of the exercise if the urge is too strong.)

The next stage is for the man to be the active partner, and the woman should lie on her front while he kneels.

- He massages her toes and legs in the same way, using oil or powder, asking her what she likes and giving her the kind of touch she requests. Again, men often use a stronger touch than women would ideally like, and should think of it more as caressing than massaging.
- Then he moves to the buttocks, back, arms, hands and neck, and strokes her hair.
- She then turns over, and he caresses her front, beginning with the feet and legs and moving to the stomach (but not the vagina), chest (but not the breasts) and arms, hands and neck.
- Again, he can touch or kiss her face, eyes, ears and mouth, but he should avoid passionate kissing at this stage.

This completes the first sensate focus exercise, and it is important that you now turn to each other, and discuss the experience. Did you lose the feeling of anxiety? Did you get to communicate physically? Was it frustrating, for both of you or just for one? Was either of you sexually aroused? What have you both learned? If it is night-time you might then go to sleep, or you may wish to stay awake and talk.

Moving on: genital sensate focus

After doing the sensate focus exercise two or three times, and assuming that your levels of anxiety have been reduced by it, you could then decide to move on to the next stage, genital sensate focus. The principle is much the same, but you may now touch the erogenous zones and stimulate each other sexually, but still avoiding orgasm. You should still begin with the sensate focus as described above, but after you have caressed the other person's front, you could move on to the man's penis and testicles, and the woman's breasts, vagina and clitoris. Again, try not to be goal-orientated, but treat it as an exercise in physical communication and anxiety reduction.

Genital Sensate Focus

- You should do exactly as you did in preparing for non-genital sensate focus, having a bath or shower, making sure the room is warm and comfortable and putting towels on the bed if you wish.
- Start with relaxation, and go on to non-genital sensate focus as before.
- Now, when you come to the front of the body, after the woman has done the non-genital massage on the man, she can touch and caress the penis and testicles.

- In the same way, after the man has done the non-genital caressing on the woman, he can touch and caress the breasts, nipples, vagina and clitoris. Remember that for many men the caressing of their nipples by the partner can be very sensual as well and so this can be part of the focus in both heterosexual and same-sex relationships.
- Again, this is not aimed at achieving an orgasm in either partner, but you should both be using a 'teasing' approach, so that when one or other of you becomes sexually aroused the active one can then stop the caressing and move to other parts of the body, or simply stop and you can talk together.

It would be all right at the end of the exercise to have an orgasm if you feel the need, either together or separately, but if it doesn't happen that is also all right, especially if the problem one of you has is difficulty in achieving an orgasm.

Problems of sexual function

We will be giving you quite a lot of information about these problems, so that you will know more about the area before you decide what to do about it. We should emphasise, however, that the complexity of the issues and the need for more thorough investigation of possible medical factors mean that you would not be able to solve many of the problems in a do-it-yourself fashion. You may therefore need to take the problem to your doctor for treatment or referral. There are now a number of sexual problem clinics in hospital psychiatry and urology departments, and also in contraception and genito-urinary medicine clinics. There are also psychosexual services in relationship and counselling organisations. There are some very effective treatments available, especially for erectile dysfunction. For many sexual problems it is therefore well worthwhile asking for professional help. There is, however, a possible advantage in making some efforts to solve the problem yourself first, because it may feel better for you to remain in control of yourself and your sex life rather than asking for external advice straight away.

How common are sexual problems?

A recent large survey in Britain reported that low sexual function is associated with increasing age, with depression, and in people who report poor health as well as for people who have less than four sexual acts in a four-week period. It is also experienced in people who find it difficult to talk easily with a partner about sex, in people who are unhappy in a relationship and in people who are ending a relationship. We will now outline in a more detailed way some of the more common and specific sexual problems.

There is limited information comparing sexual problems in men in heterosexual relationships to men who are gay. Some factors increase risk for all men such as older age and presence of anxiety or depression. Issues of body image are more likely to contribute to sexual problems for gay men. Rapid ejaculation is more common in heterosexual men.

There is less information available about the prevalence of sexual problems for lesbian women but the data currently suggests a similar pattern of prevalence. There may be some temporary changes around certain events like 'coming out' and other life-cycle events (such as leaving home and retirement).

Male sexual dysfunctions

Erectile dysfunction (ED) (impotence)

This is a problem which affects about one in ten men over-all. It is less common in younger men and usually transient whereas it is reported in about three in ten older men (over 65 years) and is more likely to remain as a chronic problem. Whilst it is reported more commonly in older men, sex remains an important part of life for many men and couples even into their eighties and nineties. There is some evidence that maintaining an active sexual life is beneficial to health overall and the risks of sexual intercourse are very low except for a small group of men who usually have a significant history of cardiovascular problems.

ED and its Treatment

- It has many possible medical causes, including diabetes mellitus, raised blood pressure, high fat and cholesterol levels in the blood, spinal cord injuries or interference with the blood supply (for example by pelvic injuries). There are many medications that can affect erection as does smoking cigarettes and consumption of higher amounts of alcohol. ED is also associated with a condition called Peyronie's disease which causes internal scarring of the penis.
- The most common two causes of erectile dysfunction are ageing and higher levels of sexual anxiety.
- Ageing is associated with a loss of sex drive, often due to low testosterone levels that may also reduce energy levels as well as cause erectile problems, and ageing is the most common reason for erectile problems in older men.
- Anxiety and stress are more common as causative factors in the younger age groups, and the erectile problem in these men is more likely to respond to psychosexual treatment or short-term use of medications.
- Psychosexual therapy is just as relevant for gay and lesbian couples as it is to those in a heterosexual relationship. Sometimes the themes may

be more focused on a specific topic. For example, in gay men there is sometimes an expectation that both men should be able to keep their erections throughout their foreplay. There may be unstated resentment or jealousy about any differences in the size of the penis and testicles or the muscularity of the body of the partner and how others may view him in comparison to the partner. Other common issues include those of minority stress, perceived risk of HIV and other infection and changes of sex roles. These themes may need careful discussion to avoid hurt and to find ways to enjoy differences between partners in a positive way.

- Psychosexual treatment would include the sensate focus approach outlined above, accompanied by helping the couple to communicate better and more freely.

- If you have a positive and enthusiastic partner, the exercises are more likely to be successful.

- A further helpful technique in the treatment of erectile problems are the Kegel exercises. These consist of contracting the muscles around the root of the penis and around the anus, so as to pull up the insides of the pelvis (similar to the movement you might make to stop the flow of urine). You should contract and relax the muscles about ten times over a period of thirty to forty seconds, and you could do this four or five times a day.

- Another related thing to remember is to keep yourself fit, by walking or doing sport, but also by smoking and drinking alcohol as little as possible.

Overall, and especially in younger men, treatment with psychosexual therapies using a cognitive and behavioural approach leads to recovery of the erectile function and maintains the improvement; but other men go on to need medication (see below).

What about medical treatment?

The treatment of erectile problems has been revolutionised in the last two decades by medications such as sildenafil (also known as Viagra), tadalafil (Cialis), vardenafil (Levitra) and avenafil (Spedra). These act as potentiators of the erectile process, and are effective in over 80 per cent of men with an erectile disorder, regardless of the exact cause. Just one thing to beware of is that if you are also on 'cardiac nitrate' drugs for heart problems, such as glyceryl trinitrate, in any form such as tablets or sprays, it would be dangerous to take drugs such as Viagra, Cialis, Levitra or Spedra at the same time as the nitrates. Specialist clinicians may also recommend the use of psychological interventions to supplement medical treatment, based on research findings of better efficacy with combined psychological interventions and medical treatment over psychological or medical treatment alone.

In those who do not respond or cannot take these drugs, there is the possibility of self-injection into the side of the penis with drugs such as Caverject or Viridal. The same drug can also be placed into the opening of the penis using a special applicator (MUSE). Another option is the use of vacuum pumps. These approaches are effective but do need more technical expertise than the Viagra-type drugs and are usually provided via specialist clinics. These clinics may conduct further investigations and in a small number of cases referral for a penile implant remains a final option.

Premature (or rapid) ejaculation (PE)

This is a very common disorder, although, because of difficulties in defining exactly who has the problem and who does not, we cannot be sure exactly how common it is. However, as definitions become more exacting, studies have found that around one in six younger men and one in ten older men complain about this problem. For some men the problem has always been present because of naturally active and sensitive reflexes when sexually aroused but for others it occurs after specific events or encounters. There are usually no specific medical causes for PE, an exception being prostatitis. In either case, PE can often become associated with ED. Problems of PE may cause distress to the man and his partner, because most women do not reach orgasm as quickly as men.

The Treatment of PE

- The use of relaxation and sensate focus exercises can be very helpful (see above).
- Some men find that they can last much longer if they ejaculate once and then have intercourse soon afterwards (making use of the refractory period – see Chapter 3).
- Kegel exercises (see above), especially learning to relax rather than contract the pelvic muscles may be useful.
- In addition, it is possible to learn the stop–start technique, in which you learn to delay ejaculation first in self-stimulation, and later in mutual sex-play with your partner. The idea is that you should approach the 'point of no return' (when ejaculation becomes inevitable), but just before you reach that point you should stop stimulating the penis and leave the feeling to subside. You will then find that you can stimulate the penis again and have more control in delaying ejaculation from then on. If this increased control can be brought into your mutual sex-play, a similar technique can be used in intercourse, with both partners stopping their movement when the point of no return is about to be reached, and then continuing after a brief delay when the urge to ejaculate has been controlled.

Other Methods for PE

- Many couples find it difficult to master this approach, and there is inconsistent evidence with regard to the effectiveness of psychological interventions for PE. As such, the combination of medical and psychosexual interventions together may be most helpful.
- In a male gay relationship, the potential advantage of having a partner who is familiar with the physical handling of their own penis and the effect of masturbating in certain positions (such as standing rather than lying down) can sometimes have a beneficial impact during the stages of therapy that involves both partners.
- A medication called dapoxetine (Priligy) is available and can increase the length of time to ejaculation, but the response does vary between individual men. The medicine has to be taken one to three hours before sexual activity. There are a number of potential side effects that will be explained by your doctor or pharmacist if this drug is considered appropriate to help you. The drug is from a group of medications called selective serotonin reuptake inhibitors (SSRI) that are commonly used for depression and anxiety.
- If dapoxetine is not effective, then some of the other SSRI medications may be prescribed on

an off-licence basis. This is because men who are prescribed SSRI medications for depression commonly report a delay to reaching ejaculation.

- The use of local anaesthetic sprays or cream is possible, but ideally should be supervised by a doctor, because it can cause numbness and may inhibit ejaculation altogether.

Delayed ejaculation

This is a much less common problem, and is estimated to occur in less than one in ten men. It is distressing when it occurs because the man is unable to obtain the pleasure of orgasm and in severe cases (if the man doesn't ejaculate at all inside the vagina) the couple may have problems with conceiving. There may be reasons for it such as the effect of neurological disorders such as spinal cord injury, or the neuropathy commonly accompanying diabetes mellitus or alcohol excess. It is a common complication of certain types of operation for prostate carcinoma, or the use of medications for depression (the SSRI group) or for prostatic hypertrophy (the alpha blockers such as tamsulosin). This problem can also be a consequence of low testosterone levels. However, in most cases no specific cause is found and it occurs because of psychological issues, insufficient stimulation or because of rather sluggish sexual reflexes.

The Treatment of Delayed Ejaculation

- The treatment of delayed ejaculation is again best done in the setting of genital sensate focus, using so-called superstimulation of the penis (by a very rapid rubbing action using body oil on the hand, either by the man himself or his partner) to achieve a greater degree of excitement and bring the man nearer to the point of no return (in other words the opposite of the treatment of PE).
- The use of a battery-powered vibrator may also be considered, to provide greater amounts of stimulation.
- There are a number of medications that may be prescribed on an off-licence basis by a specialist.
- If fertility problems occur, and/or if the problem is related to the surgical procedures for prostate hypertrophy or carcinoma, sperm retrieval to aid fertility may be possible in specialist andrology laboratories.

Female sexual dysfunctions

Problems of desire and arousal

These are not as easily divided up as the male dysfunctions, because for many women there is more commonly a combination of desire and arousal problems. Women often report that their sexuality is more bound up with emotions and their feelings about the partner than men's sexuality. Many women with a sexual problem will report a general lack of interest and arousal, although some can clearly state that it is one or the other which predominates as the problem.

Low desire is the most common complaint in women with sexual problems and it affects around one in three women. Around one in ten women report specific problems of arousal but many of these women also report problems of desire as well.

Low desire may occur in women experiencing chronic medical diseases like anaemia, diabetes mellitus, hypertension and chronic pain conditions. Hormonal problems such as low thyroid levels, low testosterone level (especially after removal of the ovaries) or high prolactin level (seen with some psychiatric medications) can lead to low sexual desire. Depression, previous trauma including physical abuse or rape, and body image disorder are also associated with problems of desire. As you may expect, many of these conditions can also cause problems with arousal and this is particularly the case with conditions such as diabetes mellitus and hypertension. Relationship problems may bring about both problems of desire and arousal.

The Treatment of Problems of Female Desire/Arousal

- Treatment approaches reflect this mix of the two conditions, and they tend to be more psychologically focused than those we use for male problems.
- There is an emphasis on the value of sex education, if possible including the partner in the therapy. It is also important to reduce any unrealistic expectations (or myths) that the woman and her partner might have, such as the idea that she is constantly ready for sex (see Chapter 3).
- It is often useful for the woman to spend some time to explore her genitals and any related sexual feelings, for example lying in a bath and exploring herself with the help of a hand-mirror. This way she may be able to become more comfortable with her own body.
- The use of lubricants (for example Sylk or Durex Sensilube), both in self-stimulation and in intercourse, is often very helpful.
- In working with the woman and her partner, the sex therapist will often also recommend the sensate focus approach (see above), which will fulfil some of the needs just mentioned.
- Controlled studies of psychotherapy have shown benefit from cognitive and behavioural therapy to improve low sexual desire and sexual

satisfaction. Mindfulness based therapy has also been shown to improve sexual desire. It is recommended that couples therapy be offered wherever possible.

- A specific vacuum device called EROS Clitoral Therapy Device is available to help some women with problems of arousal.
- There are a number of medications that may be prescribed on an off-licence basis by a specialist.

Problems of orgasm

This is more common than is generally realised, with up to one in five women reporting that they are unable to achieve an orgasm in intercourse (although many of these women can achieve an orgasm with clitoral stimulation). The belief that they should regularly experience orgasm in intercourse is probably one of the most harmful myths in the whole of sexuality. Men should be able to accept that women are different from them in this way, as in many other ways (see Chapter 3), and the wide variety of sexual expression, including the fact that many women can enjoy sex even without an orgasm, should be seen as a plus rather than a minus.

As with problems of low sexual desire and arousal, there are a number of associations with chronic medical disease states, especially those affecting neurological function such as diabetes mellitus, and conditions affecting the hormone levels in the body such as low thyroid levels and the hormonal changes in the post-menopausal years. Depression and the consequences of SSRI medications can also cause problems of reaching orgasm for women.

Our clinical experience is that the themes and topics that can bring about sexual problems between partners are extremely varied and we have attempted to ensure throughout our book that no generalisations are made that appear to stereotype issues more for one gender than the other. One common theme in lesbian couple relationships is around issues of weight and attractiveness. This may be much less important for one couple than another couple seeking help from the clinic where one woman finds it very difficult to achieve orgasm. Where it is an issue, the impact on the delivery of interventions may have to be modified. Asking one woman to explore the vulva area of her partner and to use a vibrator at varying speeds in different sites may be more playful and enjoyable when the partner is comfortable with her body weight and image. If the woman is uncomfortable, it is helpful to encourage discussion about how to adapt the exploration of the vulva to make it less anxiety provoking. Sometimes sitting together on a floor near a large mirror so that both women can see the area where the vibrator is touching the vulva can be reassuring. Ensuring the woman who is holding the vibrator tells her partner where she will be placing it before doing so and maybe finding fun ways to describe the parts of the vulva that have not been seen easily because of changes to the body shape over the years is another strategy that can be useful for some women.

The Treatment of Problems with Orgasm

- It is often easier for women to achieve orgasm in other ways than through intercourse. The most reliable ways of ensuring success using 'directed masturbation' are either by self-stimulation or with the use of a battery-powered vibrator. This is often alongside provision of sex education (and information) if required to ensure that the sexual skills training can be most effective.
- The best way to help the couple to be successful long term in achieving orgasm for the woman is by the woman teaching the man what to do for her, perhaps guiding his hand or by using the vibrator during foreplay.
- In many couples with this problem, there are also other difficulties such as low desire or lack of arousal, and a general approach is best, including sensate focus and self-exploration as above.
- If the couple can achieve an orgasm for the woman in mutual stimulation as above, they can then try incorporating some of the techniques they have used into intercourse.
- There is evidence of moderate effect in the efficacy of these treatments.

- There are a number of medications that may be prescribed on an off-licence basis by a specialist.

Vaginismus

This is a specific problem, which like the other sexual problems may co-exist with other sexual difficulties. When intercourse is attempted, although the woman may be sexually aroused, there is a tightening of the muscles around the opening of the vagina, and penetration is either very painful or impossible. This is usually associated with a strong fear of intercourse. On the other hand, sexual desire and arousal may be perfectly normal, and in foreplay or petting it may be quite easy for the woman to achieve orgasm.

The Treatment of Vaginismus

- The woman and her partner must be confident and sure of what they are doing before starting this set of interventions. It is usually recommended to start by a period of relaxation training.
- Following an internal examination by a doctor which confirms that the problem is vaginismus, and not a contraction of the pelvic muscles because of some disease state, the woman is given

a series of graded plastic 'trainers' (or tubes) to pass slowly and carefully into the vagina, using a lubricant and relaxing the muscles while doing so. The plastic tubes 'train' the vaginal muscles to relax. The woman will find that it can then get much easier to take the larger sizes, and she will soon be able to accept the larger tubes quite comfortably. ('Amielle' trainers can be obtained from Owen Mumford by mail order, see Useful addresses.)

- It may soon become possible for the woman and her partner to put fingers into the vagina without difficulty, and moving forwards they will be able to have penetration with a flaccid (soft) penis and then with an erect penis.

- Once having been successfully treated, the problem usually does not come back, so this is one of the few sexual problems which can be said to be 'cured' after therapy.

Dyspareunia (pain during intercourse)

We mention this set of problems only to say that there are many medical and gynaecological causes for it, including pelvic infections, thrush, fibroids and urinary infections (cystitis). Pain during intercourse may also be due to anxiety and difficulty in relaxing, but it would be sensible, if it has gone on for more than a few weeks, to consult your doctor and perhaps get a specialist referral.

Problems of desire (1): when the man wants sex more than the woman

In contrast to the problems of function described in the previous two sections, problems of desire are more suitable for the couple to deal with, including the 'do-it-yourself' approach. There are many couples with one partner much more interested in sex than the other. In the younger age groups it is usually the man who wants more sex than the woman, and this can be the trigger for many arguments, as well as sometimes leading him to seek outside relationships. It could then be the cause of a separation or divorce.

Sexual desire in women is usually dependent on the situation and context and is also considered relational in most circumstances rather than being a problem of performance as such. Recent changes in thinking have combined desire and arousal problems together, although this is not always the case.

Although a new drug has recently been introduced in the USA for desire disorder in women, it has so many drawbacks (such as taking it every day and having to avoid any alcohol) that few women and their physicians have started to use it. There is also the concern that many women may feel they have to take a tablet to prevent any likelihood of anger, threats or actual violence from their partner, or the concern the partner may stray outside the monogamous relationship. Also in discussion by our team many of us felt that it was only trying to treat a symptom rather than resolve any underlying problems. As such, it is likely that psychological ways of helping couples resolve their issues will remain the best treatment option for the foreseeable future.

When is it likely to happen?

There are some stages in the relationship in which the problem is more likely to occur. For example, when the woman has recently had a baby, she may be 'off' sex for many reasons:

- Physical pain following the delivery
- Disturbed nights
- The responsibility of baby care
- The fact that breastfeeding offers a different kind of physical and emotional satisfaction
- Resentment at the man's 'selfishness'

At other stages of the relationship, there are different sources of tension and anger which can reduce a woman's interest in sex:

- Worry about the children
- Competing demands of homemaking and career
- Upset over a bereavement
- Time to study or training for a new career in the evening
- Time for self to relax
- Caring for elderly parents

Relationship factors involved

The relationship itself may be adding to the problems, and in the 'reluctant woman' situation this is often because she is overshadowed by the man, who makes all the important decisions and doesn't allow her to be an equal partner. Sometimes the woman may accept the pressure for sex, but seem not to be enjoying it, and sometimes she will refuse to take part in sex at all. The man may assume, as men often do, that his partner must be ill or disturbed because he believes that women 'should want and enjoy sex as much as men' (see Chapter 3). In some couples the woman will accept this theory, and even go to her doctor asking for treatment to increase her sex drive, a treatment which, even if the doctor goes along with it, is unlikely to work.

Finding a compromise for how often sex happens

In order to find a way forwards with this problem, it is very important for you both to agree that neither of you is abnormal, and that each person has his or her own sexual needs. There may be a good deal of progress to be made in having some discussions about any resentments that the woman may have. It is also possible to help her to get more enthusiastic about sex by asking her what parts of the sexual experience she enjoys and how it could be made more attractive to her.

However, one of the best ways of tackling this problem is for you both to agree on a compromise frequency for sex to take place. It may sound slightly crazy to do this, but if neither of you is abnormal, it makes sense for both of you to give way a little. So, for example, if the man would like sex to take place three times a week and the woman would prefer once every two weeks, you might settle for sex once a week. This is the beginning, but not the end of the story, and you need to be a bit more specific in your planning, as follows.

The timetable

The agreement on how often sex should take place has the possibility of satisfying both partners. The man may be content that it would provide an acceptable level of sex for his needs, and the woman may be reassured that she would not be overwhelmed by his demands. This compromise, however, does not solve the problem on its own, because there might be a fresh dispute every day as to whether today was the day for sex or not.

- A good way to overcome this problem is for the couple to agree on a timetable (see Chapter 6) determining on which days of the week sex would take place.
- So, for example, it might be agreed that sex would happen on Fridays only, and not on any other days.
- The woman would then know that she will not be pressured on other days, and the man knows that sex will be happening on a regular basis on Fridays without any conflict.

The disadvantage is that the spontaneity is taken out of sex, and some couples may feel that they cannot use the technique for that reason. However, if you think about the initiation of sex, it is usually only one partner who has the idea, and who then persuades the other one that it would be a nice thing to do. This makes it unspontaneous for the second partner, and thus spontaneity is not total or mutual in the first place. It could therefore be something that as a couple you feel that you could sacrifice, for the sake of an arrangement that works and also takes the heat out of your conflict over sex.

The timetable may be enhanced for some couples whereby the woman requests something else which would be nice for her on the agreed day for sex, so that it does not all appear to be solely about sex and for him. Likewise, on one of the other six days the man may choose to ask for something else that is nice for him. It may be important to reach agreement up-front about the possibility for self-stimulation on non-sex days so there does not develop any resentment if either one finds their partner masturbating.

What about unforeseen difficulties with the days?

This might depend on whose side the problem was on. If, for example, the woman is unable to have sex on the arranged day because of her period, she should propose an alternative day. If, however, the man is away at a golf tournament, he should probably miss his 'sex day' for that week. You may have to make a set of rules to cover this kind of eventuality.

How long will the timetable have to be continued?

The timetable may bring so much relief that you feel you want to continue with it for a long time. If it is working well, however, it may have improved your relationship sufficiently for you to go back to spontaneous sex without conflict. A good way to test this is to suspend the timetable for a week or two (again by consultation together) and then see whether it is better to continue with it or to go back to spontaneity again. Some couples have continued with it for months or even years, and see no reason to give it up.

CASE EXAMPLE

Leslie (41) and his wife Heidi (39) had been married for ten years and had a nine-year-old daughter. They had been having relationship and sexual problems for four years. These began when Leslie had to change his career after being laid off, and became rather depressed. He went into counselling, but also began to lean on Heidi, and was asking for reassurance more than before. At this time, Heidi began to go off sex (which she had previously enjoyed), partly because of Leslie's increased dependency on her. He was upset by this, and pressured her for sex on most days. Sex actually happened once a month on average. In therapy they agreed to try a timetable for sex to take place on Wednesdays. They also agreed that Leslie would bring coffee to Heidi on Sunday mornings, and look after their daughter so that Heidi could sleep late. The arrangement was very successful, and some months later they were still using the timetable, with weekly satisfactory sex, and a generally improved relationship.

In the case of Leslie and Heidi above, it is useful to note that we asked him to take over some of the 'looking after' that she had mainly been responsible for up to that point, balancing the relationship as well as directly altering the sexual interaction.

Problems of desire (2): when the woman wants sex more than the man

This is in some ways the opposite side of the coin, but has things in common with the previous problem. The couple who experience this problem are often older, and the man is possibly entering the stage of life when sex is not an overwhelming priority for him. It may also be a second marriage for him, and his wife may be somewhat younger. In any event, the problem as presented is that she is keen to have sex frequently and he is reluctant. The timetable would be a theoretical possibility, but is not so easily adapted to this situation because, while the woman can allow sex to happen even if she is not completely committed to it, for the man this is more difficult. He would probably worry that he would be unable to get an erection if he were to agree to sex on a particular day of the week. There may be some exceptions, but it is probably better to use an alternative strategy if this is your problem.

The need for assertiveness on his side

We have found in our couple therapy clinics that many men with this problem are diplomatic, unassertive and hate to argue. This is in contrast to their partners, who are often outspoken, emotionally expressive and open. The man is therefore at a disadvantage. He is good at keeping the peace, but he tends to lose most of the couple's arguments, and he may build up some resentment. It is a good example of the 'attack and withdraw' couple whom we described in Chapter 4. The problem is at its worst when the couple are arguing about sex. The female partner is outspoken on this subject, blaming the male for his lack of sex drive and initiative, and the quiet man usually agrees that she is right, even though he may have his private reservations. The outcome is that they seldom get around to having sex because he is always somewhat resentful, although he would never admit it. He may also be afraid of her criticism if the process goes wrong, for example if he ejaculates early or if she fails to get the pleasure she expects.

What to do about it: argue about something trivial

It will be seen from the example below that it may be possible to improve the situation by encouraging him to argue a little more strongly, and to help her to understand that her strength in argument can undermine her interests in the sexual area. It is very much like the exercise that we suggested in Chapter 6, in which you sit together and argue about something quite trivial such as the dirty clothes or the toothpaste tube. The important thing to remember in these arguments is that the quieter (male) partner should go on arguing even when he thinks he ought to give in for the sake of peace, and that the more outspoken (female) partner should deliberately encourage him to speak out and 'hold his own' in the argument.

CASE EXAMPLE

Brian (53) and Stella (51) had been married for twenty-five years, and their children had left home. The problem was that Stella complained bitterly and frequently that Brian never wanted sex with her, in spite of a previous course of treatment involving sensate focus (see above). Brian was quiet and diplomatic, and never disagreed with Stella. In the third session of therapy, we asked him whether there was any small thing on which he had a difference of opinion with her. After some hesitation he said that sometimes he felt she was too fussy about the toilet seat: he thought it did not matter whether it was left up or down, while she was insistent that it should be left down. They had a lively argument about it, the liveliest argument they had had in their whole marriage. We encouraged him not to give in too quickly, and they finally 'agreed to differ'. Later in that week they had intercourse at his instigation, and from then on their sex life became more regular, and Stella expressed more respect for him in many other aspects of their marriage.

A word of warning

These arguments are often therapeutic for the couple if they go well and both partners can take part in them in a fairly light-hearted manner. If, however, you have a relationship which is characterised by conflict and there have been violent episodes in the past, it might be safer not to try to have trivial arguments. It would also be wise, in any case, when having these kind of arguments, to make sure that you have not drunk alcohol or taken other substances on that day: these could reduce inhibitions too much and increase the risk of arguments getting out of hand.

Alternative strategies for sexual desire problems

There is much that can be done for the sexual desire problems outlined above, without resorting to either timetables or arguments.

- You can certainly use the sensate focus approach in both male and female desire problems, and there is no reason why these exercises should not work.
- There is also the idea of simply increasing the openness of your communication (see Chapter 5), which again should help the problem in a general way.
- Any resentments that either partner feels could be explored in a timed discussion, as outlined in Chapter 5, and this should lead to an improvement in the general relationship, which may help the sexual relationship.

> • It also helps some couples to watch explicit or erotic videos together. This is not necessarily a long-term solution, but it may be able to break the silence and help you to talk about sex in a more constructive way, as well as having an immediate positive effect on sexual interest.

When to seek outside help

There is never any harm in trying to improve your relationship using the techniques we have outlined in this chapter, and it should probably be your first option whatever you decide to do later. However, sexual desire problems are not always easy to resolve, and many couples have found that they are unable to improve the situation without professional help. We have given a list in Useful addresses of some of the resources available in both couple relationship work and in sexual therapy and counselling. There are several ways to arrange counselling or treatment. If it is primarily a non-sexual problem or a problem of sexual motivation only, it would be quite sensible to ask for therapy or counselling from a couple counselling organisation or clinic that deals with these problems. If it is a problem of sexual function (for example an erectile problem, vaginismus or dyspareunia) it would probably be best to seek advice first from your doctor, followed by a referral to a clinic that specialises in these problems.

Key Points

- Sexual drive, sexual desire, sexual arousal and orgasm are all defined.
- Advice is given on how to discuss sexual difficulties.
- It's important to keep expectations realistic.
- Relaxation and sensate focus exercises are described.
- Advice is given on how to deal with erectile disorder, premature ejaculation and delayed ejaculation.
- Advice is given on how to deal with desire/arousal disorder in women, and with problems of orgasm, vaginismus and dyspareunia.
- In couples where the man is keener on sex than the woman, the timetable may be used.
- In couples where the woman is keener on sex than the man, having trivial arguments may be considered.
- In many cases it will be necessary to seek medical help or counselling for the sexual problem.

8

In sickness and in health

Introduction

In this chapter we are dealing with issues which some readers will find painful, and perhaps would rather not know about. On the other hand, other readers, who have encountered these illnesses, will be thinking that it's about time that someone wrote about them. We will be referring first to physical illnesses, and then to psychiatric illnesses, psychological problems and problem drinking, with advice about how to cope with them as a couple. The illnesses will undoubtedly cause stress, but in most cases it is better to think about these problems in advance, so as not to be completely bowled over if something then happens which we have to cope with as an emergency.

Couples and physical illness

The couple relationship is of course one which can be highly satisfying and can provide a lifelong support system for both partners and for their children. However, there is always the risk that sooner or later one or the other will fall ill, more commonly in later life, and this usually has to be dealt with primarily by the partner who remains well. Whatever the illness, this partner will have to take on more responsibilities, and there will also be a change in the balance of power in the relationship. These are some of the long-term physical illnesses which can result in stress on the partner:

- Heart disease (especially coronary disease)
- Cancer
- Diabetes and other metabolic disorders
- Kidney disease (including renal dialysis and transplants)
- Physical disabilities (including wheelchair cases)
- Neurological diseases (e.g. multiple sclerosis and strokes)
- Epilepsy
- Problems after surgery and accidents

It is often tempting for the well partner (the carer) to take over completely in these circumstances, but that isn't necessarily the best route to take. The ill partner should be encouraged to do as much for themselves and for the other partner as they reasonably can, to give them a better self-image and to reduce the burden on the carer. The couple should try to form a 'health alliance' to find out as much as they can about the illness, and combine forces to get the best out of the health services. There are also support groups that can be accessed by them to help the ill partner to meet others with the condition, and the well partner to meet other carers. It is also helpful (depending on their ages) to keep children informed about the illness and its possible consequences, so that the developments don't come as a surprise to them.

How do these illnesses affect the relationship?

All these illnesses affect not only the sufferers themselves but also their partners and other family members. There is not a great deal of research on the effects of illness on partners and families, but in our clinical experience a partner's illness can have quite severe repercussions, including depression in the 'well' partner. The response of the partner is a significant factor both in how the sufferer copes with the illness and how the family as a whole responds to the stress of the situation.

Acceptance of the illness

Both the patient and the partner/carer have to accept the reality of the illness, and take a realistic view of what the future condition of the patient is likely to be. This may take time, and it is important that the partners talk about the problems on a fairly regular basis, with input from their doctors or surgeons. It is also helpful to be able to discuss the illness with friends and relatives, so as not to hide it under a cloud of secrecy.

Equalisation wherever possible

The aim should always be to encourage the ill person to be a fully participating partner in couple and family life, as long as their health allows it. Both they and the partner have to be constantly aware of the changing situation as the illness progresses, and at every stage reach the best adjustment in terms of what each partner contributes.

Effect on the partner who remains well

Some well partners can become quite stressed by the illness and the extra burdens that they need to take on as a result. Here the ill partner can have a role to play in reassuring the well one that they are doing all that can be done under the difficult circumstances that they face. Doctors, surgeons and healthcare workers are gradually becoming more aware of the stresses that partners face, and will in some cases provide or arrange counselling for them.

Couples and psychiatric illnesses

Similar problems face the partners of those who suffer psychiatric illnesses, and here there is a further stress in that the illnesses carry a stigma, which means they may not be understood by friends, relatives or neighbours. The more common psychiatric illnesses include:

- Depression and anxiety
- Schizophrenia and other paranoid states
- Manic depressive (bipolar) disorder
- Dementia (including Alzheimer's disease)
- The consequences of brain injuries and strokes

We will deal in some detail with depression, schizophrenia and manic depressive illness, which present more specific problems for the partner, but are also amenable to strategies that the couple can use to alleviate their difficulties. We will then go on to mention briefly a number of similar conditions which can affect the relationship, including dementia, brain injuries and strokes.

The importance of 'normalisation'

It is always best to work together to get medical help, including medication, as soon as possible. There is effective medication and 'talking therapy' available for many of the illnesses, and in addition this can be supplemented by some well-tried methods which the relatives and partners can use to help the sufferer to overcome their disorder and live a more normal life (see below). The most useful message that the sufferer and their partner can hear is that, whatever the illness, it is possible to get over the problems and have a reasonably satisfying life in spite of them. It is also helpful to think of the sufferer not as 'a schizophrenic' or 'a depressive', but as someone who suffers from schizophrenia or depression. This reminds us that the sufferer is firstly a human being and secondly an ill person, and hopefully increases the chances that they will be able to live a more normal life.

The role of the carer

Whenever someone becomes psychiatrically ill there is a disturbance in the balance within their relationship. The person who is ill or stressed has to some extent become weaker or more vulnerable than they were before, and often their partner or another relative has to take over some of their duties and responsibilities. If the person who is ill recognises that they have a problem, it is easier to cope with this transition, but if they have no 'insight' it becomes more difficult, and may lead to disputes about how much they can be trusted to do.

Depression

Depression is a very common problem, and almost always affects the partner as well as the sufferer. Often the depressed partner experiences a loss of self-esteem and confidence. The 'well' partner has to take over some of the responsibilities of the ill partner, and may have to take care of them if they are in any way dangerous to themselves. It is important to make sure that the depressed partner is not experiencing suicidal thoughts, and if they are, then an urgent appointment at a psychiatric unit should be arranged.

What to do about it: self-help using cognitive and other forms of psychotherapy

Depression should be taken seriously, and the depressed person should be encouraged, if the problem persists for long, to consult their doctor and if necessary get referred to a hospital for treatment, which should include medication and/or psychological therapy (see below). There is however also the possibility of self-help treatment using cognitive behavioural techniques as described in another book in this series, *Overcoming Depression* by Paul Gilbert, and it would be sensible for both partners firstly to try to apply some of the ideas in that book within the relationship. These include pinpointing 'trigger' events, feelings or images that may lead to depressed thinking, and challenging the negative thoughts that result. It would then still be possible to go for more formal therapy if this was thought to be necessary.

Increased sensitivity in the depressed partner

The depressed person is generally sensitive to criticism, and the 'well' partner may have to be careful what they say. This doesn't mean that argument is necessarily a bad thing, but the well partner has to be more circumspect in an argument, realising that the 'ill' partner may be hypersensitive in many areas of life compared with the way they were before the depression started.

Keeping the 'ill' partner more active

It often seems that a vicious cycle develops in depression, in that the patient becomes inactive, perhaps having to be off work or otherwise missing out on normal activities. It can improve matters if they can be encouraged to do more things, even if sometimes they don't seem to want to. A diary of daily activities can help to show if progress is being made, and both partners can monitor how things are improving. Simple exercise can also be helpful in increasing fitness and improving morale.

What about sex?

Often a depressed person is less interested in sex than before, and the partner should be aware of this. It may cause conflict, but it may be possible to deal with it (as we suggested in Chapter 7) by discussion, by setting up a timetable or by agreeing on a temporary pause in this side of the relationship. In some cases, however, the depressed partner's sex drive is not actually reduced at all, but the well partner may think that it would be wrong to raise the topic, and in that case an open and sympathetic discussion may resolve the issue.

What if the problem really lies in the relationship?

In some couples, however, the depression is not necessarily a clinical problem, but more of a reaction to difficulties in communication. The partner designated as the 'patient' may have slipped into a passive and withdrawn way of reacting to a dominant and possibly intrusive partner (see Chapter 6), and may therefore seem to be showing signs of 'depression'. It is always worth asking the question as to whether the 'depression' gets worse when the couple are together, and whether they could do anything to alter it by treating each other differently. If you find yourself in this situation, it is well worth having a timed discussion (see Chapter 5) with an agenda to see whether the non-depressed partner is doing anything to make the depression worse, because they could then do something to improve it.

CASE EXAMPLE

Jane (38) and Joseph (40) had been married for twenty years, with a sixteen-year-old son. The original pre-senting problem was that Jane, an active and go-ahead marketing executive, had been suffering from stress and a degree of depression for the past two years, although she had benefited from cognitive therapy. One of her main worries, however, was that Joseph was 'stuck in a rut' in his work (as a self-employed antique dealer) and that he was 'deeply depressed' about it. She spent much of her time worrying about him and thinking about how he could improve his situation, and had drawn up several action plans, all of which he rejected as being unrealistic. In couple therapy it emerged that his 'depressions' were not as severe as she thought, and a helpful intervention was when the therapist suggested that she should stop worrying about him, and that his 'bad days' were not the result of depression but of his perfectionistic personality and the current trough in the market. She became more relaxed about the situation, and the tensions between them decreased considerably. Joseph never took anti-depressants, but his attitude to his problems became more optimistic as Jane took less notice of them. Her depression was relieved by the reduction in the marital tensions and her own cognitive therapy.

Getting help: antidepressants

Antidepressant drugs are often very helpful in treating depression, although they are not actually 'happiness pills'. They act more as a kind of 'extra skin' psychologically, enabling the patient to accept the stresses and disappointments of life without getting too upset about them. They control the condition rather than curing it, but episodes of depression are in any case often fairly short-lasting, and some patients should be able to discontinue medication fairly soon after starting it.

Getting help: cognitive behavioural therapy, couple therapy and psychodynamic therapy

There are also now a number of clinics in which it is possible to obtain cognitive behavioural therapy, couple therapy or psy-chodynamic psychotherapy for depression. You might think of this if you prefer not to take medication, if you have had a poor response to it, or if the depression seems to have gone on for a long time. The methods used may produce results which are longer-lasting than the effects of antidepressants.

Schizophrenia and bipolar (manic depressive) disorder

(In a short self-help book we are not intending to give a lot of space to these more serious mental illnesses. However, some knowledge about the way that couple therapy can help these disorders might be useful to you in dealing with more everyday problems in your partner.)

Schizophrenia

This is a condition which typically starts in the teens or twenties and can either run a variable course with periods of illness and periods of being well, or may result in a long-term illness which lasts for life. There are many types of symptoms, but in most cases the patient has false beliefs (delusions), often of a persecutory or grandiose nature, and may also hear voices. With the help of medication the illness can be made much milder, but it is unusual for a complete cure to be achieved.

How is the relationship affected?

Schizophrenia obviously affects the relationship quite radically. The first crisis is usually that of admission to the hospital. Here the patient may not be aware ('lack of insight') that they have an illness, and may want to act on the delusions, perhaps doing things that endanger themselves or others. In the face of this behaviour, the nearest relative (often the partner) has to make the decision to bring in the doctor and social worker to see whether the patient needs to be hospitalised against their will. The professional team will certainly make it clear to the patient and partner what the consequences will be.

What happens after discharge from the hospital?

Here we enter the world of rehabilitation, in which the ill partner is helped to readjust to outside life following a breakdown. Research has shown that in schizophrenia the chances of a good recovery are increased by regular medication. The patient is further helped if the partner (or nearest relative) is calm, quiet and low-key in their approach, rather than enthusiastic or pushy. It also helps if the patient has (as in the case of depression, above) some interesting and rewarding activity during the day. If they can return to their old job this is ideal. Even if they cannot return to work, it is a good idea for them to be out and about for some time every day, to keep from getting too stuck in the rather inactive way of life that the illness sometimes causes such patients to lead. The recommendation from research is also that the patient should not spend more than thirty-five hours per week in face-to-face contact with the nearest relative. In the longer term it is quite possible for the ill partner to return to something like equality within the relationship, and again it helps if they can find an area they can take the lead in, for example gardening or helping the children with homework.

Manic depressive (bipolar) disorder

In this condition there are unpredictable periods of either high or low moods, and the breakdowns are usually fairly short-lasting, taking the form of either severe depressive episodes, with suicidal ideas, or manic behaviour, with grandiose ideas and impulsivity. In either of these states the patient may need to be hospitalised against their will (see above), because of the danger to themselves or others, but the periods of illness will usually resolve quite quickly, and there are long periods of normality between them. There is a range of effective medications which can both damp down the severity of the manic behaviour and the depressive episodes and protect against recurrences. The role of the partner is to remain vigilant for the early signs of a breakdown, to ensure rapid treatment if one occurs and to protect the patient and family from any danger resulting from the illness.

Dementia, strokes and brain injury

The role of the partner in these conditions is somewhat similar to that in schizophrenia and manic depressive illness. There is of course a wide variety of problem behaviours that affect such patients, but in most cases the partner has to deal with the patient's unpredictability and loss of memory. The partner may need to be responsible for many aspects of the patient's life, such as helping to set up reminders in the home for their daily activities, or arranging for professional home care to prevent dangerous situations. It is not always possible to persuade the patient to go into long-term residential care, even if the medical advisors advocate it. Sometimes it is possible to obtain respite care in a similar setting to those providing long-term care, and this can take the pressure off the partner for a short period. It may then be possible to persuade the reluctant patient that longer-term residential care would be a good solution.

Stress and psychological problems affecting the relationship

There are a number of problems which can affect individuals and can have a strong influence on the relationship, but which are not necessarily defined as psychiatric. These include general anxieties and worries, as well as work-related stress, which can cause considerable pressure on the partner because of the need to reassure the worrying partner or to reason with them about their fears. The response to this should be to discuss the situation, if necessary on a timed basis, and see if any solution can be found to the stresses themselves. In this process the couple may be more effective working as a team than as individuals.

Jealousy

This is a problem which is especially relevant to couple relationships, because the jealous ideas centre around the partner. It may involve repeated interrogation about what the partner has been doing and who they might have been meeting, and sometimes even detective work such as phoning the partner unexpectedly, questioning their friends and searching their belongings.

The jealousy may of course be delusional, part of a paranoid psychosis akin to schizophrenia. In this situation there may be some degree of danger to the partner, and the solution may have to involve either separation of the partners or psychiatric treatment, or both.

However, the more common kind of jealousy, which is more like an exaggeration of the normal possessiveness within couples (see Chapter 4), may be associated with mild depression, with insecurity – or alcohol misuse – (see below) or with stress. Here it is possible to use couple therapy to help the problem, and in some cases the problem may be able to be dealt with on a self-help basis, as we will show in the next section.

How to deal with it: increase communication

Very often jealousy is based on a misunderstanding between the two partners, for example if the non-jealous partner does things innocently, like being friendly with colleagues, which the jealous partner misinterprets as indicating infidelity. If it becomes clear that this is so, a timed discussion session (see Chapter 5) may give the couple the possibility of increasing their empathy for each other, to the extent that the springs of the jealousy are no longer so powerful. Knowing how the problem arises, the non-jealous partner may be able to reduce their natural sociability or flirtatiousness out of respect for the sensitivities of the jealous partner, and so control the problem.

How to deal with it: the jealousy timetable

If it is not possible to change the situation by improved communication and changed behaviour, more creative solutions may have to be sought. The jealousy timetable is something which we developed in our couple therapy clinic, and it is based on the idea that jealous accusations may be difficult to suppress, but they can be made bearable if they can be time-limited. So, if the jealous partner can't stop the accusations and the interrogation, it may still be possible to keep them under control if you agree to speak together openly about the issue, with full cooperation on both sides, but only at a specified time each day. The exercise below will make it clearer how you should go about it. A similar approach may be used for other types of behaviour in one partner (for example, complaining about the partner in a repetitive way – see Chapter 6) which are difficult to stop doing and which the partner finds unbearable. The timetable should give the complaining partner a chance to have the other's full attention during the specified time, and the other partner will be reassured that they don't have to put up with it all day.

The Jealousy Timetable

- Recognise that the jealous partner needs to talk about their jealous thoughts from time to time.
- The jealous partner should acknowledge that when this happens it is painful and difficult for the other partner.
- You should then agree on how much time it is reasonable to spend talking about these ideas – a good compromise might be once a day for thirty minutes.
- You should plan to sit down with the timer going and no distractions for thirty minutes once a day at a planned time (e.g. 9 p.m.), and you will then talk about nothing else but the jealous ideas.
- During this time the non-jealous partner will give the other one his/her full attention and answer all questions.
- If the subject of jealousy comes up at any other time earlier in the day, the non-jealous partner should say 'I can't discuss that now but we have thirty minutes at 9 p.m. and we will deal with it fully at that time'.

Again, if this is not successful it would be worth seeking either counselling as a couple or individual therapy for the jealous individual.

Alcohol and other substance abuse

These are problems which have a profound influence on the relationship, and the partner will usually be well aware of the need for treatment. However, the drug or alcohol user needs to be motivated to seek treatment, and in many cases they are not even convinced that they have a problem. Treatment can't be forced on an unwilling patient.

Alcohol and its influence on the relationship

Alcohol can be a very good social lubricant, and many couples first meet in a situation in which alcohol is being served, such as at a bar or a party. It can also in small doses be quite helpful in reducing inhibitions. However, being dependent upon, or misusing alcohol (drinking to excess, with or without a true state of addiction) is a common problem, more so in men than in women, affecting perhaps 5 per cent of the population in the West. Dependency upon or misuse of alcohol can have a devastating effect on the relationship and on family life. Intoxication with alcohol has several effects on the relationship:

- It makes the drinking partner more impatient, demanding and insensitive.

- It leaves the non-drinking partner with the responsibility of dealing with an unpredictable situation.
- It costs money, which usually comes from the family accounts.
- The drinking partner may be sexually demanding but often unable to perform.
- The drinking partner may become violent (see Chapter 9).
- The non-drinking partner is likely to become resentful and reject the drinker.

This sometimes leads to a very unequal kind of relationship, with the drinker taking the role of the irresponsible sinner and the other partner the role of the saint. In extreme cases, the drinker is hardly aware of anything outside his or her need for the next drink, and then the couple relationship takes a very low priority in their thinking.

Coping with moderate problem drinking as a couple

The problems raised by alcohol are complex, and it is not often possible to solve them by self-help couple work on its own. The only exception is in those couples where the drinking is at a fairly early stage, and the drinking partner is not really dependent upon, or misusing alcohol. There is therefore still some control over the drinking, and the drinking may sometimes be in response to strains in the relationship. You may in this situation decide that you can get together to have a timed discussion of the problems and work out what the particular areas of stress might be that are contributing to the problem. However, it is better in these discussions to use ordinary everyday tasks, such as help with the children or coming home on time, rather than tackling the more sensitive issue of drinking. By this means it may be possible to improve the general relationship to the point that the drinker can control their drinking.

Coping with excessive drinking

When drinking gets so extreme that the drinker is hiding bottles, drinking in the mornings to start the day and having periods of amnesia when drunk, there is obviously a problem which is too severe to be solved by couple discussions. There is only one way out in the end, and this is for the drinker to receive help to achieve abstinence (since unfortunately 'social drinking' as an option is only successful in about 5 per cent of those who are dependent upon, or misusing alcohol). This help may be provided by Alcoholics Anonymous, with the well-known 'twelve step' programme for achieving abstinence, or it may be obtained through the various NHS or private clinics which offer 'drying out' treatments followed by help with maintaining abstinence. There is also help for partners and relatives of those who are dependent upon, or misusing alcohol from Alanon, and the organisation Children of Alcoholics offers help to those whose parents are problem drinkers.

Drug abuse within the relationship

The problems posed by drug abuse are in some ways similar to those which arise from alcohol abuse, but depending on the particular drug being used the results may differ. Mild degrees of addiction can be triggered and maintained by problems in the relationship, and couple discussions can sometimes help. More severe addiction, however, will, like being dependent upon, or misusing alcohol, take over the user's whole life, and there is little that can be done besides enrolling in a drug withdrawal and treatment programme, either through a clinic or an organisation like Narcotics Anonymous.

- Marijuana smoking is often done on a social basis, with both partners involved. It can, however, especially with the stronger preparations such as 'skunk' and 'spice', reach problem proportions, with the user being almost permanently under the influence of the drug, and possibly suffering from paranoid ideas as a result. Then it needs more than a discussion as a couple to resolve the problems, and drug addiction programmes may be needed.

- Drugs like heroin, which lead to sedation when they are used and severe withdrawal symptoms when the user is deprived of them (known as going 'cold turkey'), cause a great deal of disruption in the relationship; and the user, like those who are extremely dependent upon, or misusing alcohol, is thinking most of the time about how to get the next 'fix'. Usually there is little that can be done by the couple about the drug habit without professional help.
- Cocaine, like marijuana, is a drug which can be used socially, but especially in its 'crack' form it becomes very addictive, and the user, as with alcohol or heroin, lives for nothing but the next dose of crack. The partner is of course severely affected by the drug habit, but can do little about it without the help of a professional drug clinic or treatment service.

Conclusions

When a partner is physically ill, psychiatrically ill, psychologically disturbed or has a substance abuse problem, there is always an imbalance in the relationship and a degree of stress on the other partner, who has to take on extra responsibility. It is sometimes possible for a couple with one of the partners unwell to do something to alleviate the stresses, and thereby perhaps to hasten recovery from the problem, or, if it is not treatable, to make it easier to cope with. The situation may actually lead to a strengthening of the bond between the partners and help them to grow as individuals.

Key Points

- Illnesses in one partner are very common.
- They affect the other partner, sometimes even more than the ill one.
- It is best to try to give the ill partner the chance to live as normal a life as possible.
- The couple should work together to find out as much as they can about the illness.
- Social stigma causes more difficulties with psychiatric or addiction problems than with physical illnesses.
- There is much that both partners can do to alleviate the stress of illness, to cope with it more effectively and live a satisfying life in spite of it.

9

Domestic abuse and violence

The nature of the problem

There is much written about domestic abuse and violence. This is not limited to physical assault from a man to a woman and can take many different formats. Domestic abuse is any incident of threatening behaviour, including violence, and can include abuse of any type. Typically, this can be psychological, emotional, financial, sexual as well as or without physical violence. The abuse can occur in any type of intimate relationship. Violence is often regarded simply as criminal behaviour that is the result of one person's violent temperament, and that it is unconnected with the relationship between the two people involved. However, the position is often more complicated than that, and there are many possible factors leading to fights and physical beatings within the relationship. Each case of domestic violence is unique, with a mix of factors leading to the violent events. These may include:

- The traditional view that men, as the dominant partners, have the right to chastise their wives (perhaps more common in those from Asian and African countries – see Chapter 1).
- An inbuilt tendency of men to be violent. This may have implications when two gay men in a relationship get into a fight and where both feel it is important to be able to demonstrate who is the strongest man.
- Some men's dominating and sadistic behaviour, sometimes amounting to 'coercive control'.
- The social isolation of the couple, leading to the man 'getting away' with violence, or
- An escalation of 'normal' conflict between partners (perhaps fuelled by alcohol) leading to violence.

The police forces have special protection units that are sometimes called the Community Safety Unit. These units have dedicated teams that deal with crimes of domestic abuse, rape and other sexual assaults, as well as 'honour based' violence. If you should ever feel that a situation may escalate out of control and that you feel unsafe, then make sure you familiarise yourself with how to withdraw from the situation safely, taking any other vulnerable people, including children, with you if at all possible. We will come back to this later in the chapter.

It is worth mentioning that forced marriage became an offence in 2014 (in England and Wales) and continues to target four times as many women as men. Forced marriages are different from arranged marriages where each person has the choice to accept the arrangement or not. Domestic abuse includes that which occurs within forced marriages. Support for anyone in such a relationship can be found from the local Community Safety Unit.

Is separation the only way to deal with it?

In many discussions of domestic violence, the conclusion is reached that the only way to help is to remove the woman and her children from the abusive male partner. There is indeed good reason in many cases to protect the partner who has become the victim. It is always right for her (since it is usually the woman who is in the position of having to ask for help in a violent situation) to have the possibility to find refuge if necessary. However, unless you are in a situation where the man has started to resort to physical violence to control his female partner, it is always worth considering whether both partners can think of the violence as a regrettable outcome of the struggle between the two partners, and therefore trying to tackle it by helping the couple to live together more peacefully and safely.

Violence between partners

Around a quarter of all women and a sixth of all men

experience some form of domestic abuse sometime in their life. For many women, this is likely to be experienced on a more frequent basis and is typically more severe in nature. Unfortunately, only a small minority of incidents ever reach public knowledge. Physical violence between partners is very common. In many cases the violence is described by one or both partners as relatively minor, and it gets passed over as a 'blip' in an otherwise satisfactory relationship. On the other hand, among couples coming to therapy or counselling, there is a high level of violence reported – up to 30 per cent of couples in one study. The usual trigger is an argument between the partners, and usually there is an escalation of conflict, involving firstly an ordinary argument, then raised voices with name-calling, and finally the physical fight. This may involve pushing, shoving and slapping, or damage to objects, and only rarely would it escalate to punching or kicking.

The domestic violence disclosure scheme

Introduced in 2014, this scheme, also known as Clare's Law, allows members of the public to approach the police if they have a concern that their partner may pose a risk to them. It is also possible for a third person to approach and inform the police if there is concern that someone they know may pose a risk to their partner. Sometimes other people will see actions or behaviours in a different light to the person most closely involved with the individual. The police can check for any history of previous abuse and may share the information with the partner(s) to help that person make a more informed decision about whether to continue in a relationship. They can also provide help and support in making the choice. The information is always given in person and no documentation is given to the person. Sometimes, by addressing the matter early in the relationship, the use by the couple of some of the exercises we have shared in Chapters 4, 5 and 6 can be very helpful in preventing an escalation of violence.

The dangerous consequences

Research has shown that women are just as likely to begin a physical conflict as men, and that they participate equally in the more minor activities such as pushing. It is not only in heterosexual relationships that violence occurs; there is some quite serious violence in same-sex relationships too. Indeed, in gay male relationships there can be a dangerous escalation of violence which can lead to serious injuries. However, in heterosexual relationships men are usually physically stronger than women, and more used to fighting, so that if it comes to a serious fight between the two, the man usually inflicts more damage. In the worst cases this can result in serious injury, and in a significant number of cases it results in death. If you are concerned about the escalation of violence against you and you feel that this will not stop, then you should consider making a criminal allegation against your partner to the police. The allegation will be investigated and your partner may be arrested. If the police consider you to be at risk and in need of protection, then they will act immediately.

Winning and losing

There is another factor which affects the situation, and that is that, as we mentioned in Chapter 3, women have verbal skills which are not always matched by their male partner. If the conflict were to remain only at the verbal level, it is probable that the woman would usually 'win', and the man would be reduced to agreeing with her opinions most of the time. Many men, however, feel humiliated by a situation in which their partners end by having the last word and getting their way in everything. They have the 'ultimate weapon' of being physically stronger, and may be tempted to use this if they seem to be losing out in the power struggle.

Alcohol as a factor

A further factor in the situation is the use of alcohol. This applies mainly to men, and in one study it was shown that men who were violent in their relationships were more likely to be drinking after work, drinking at home in the evenings, drinking while looking after the children and drinking during recreational activities, compared with men who were non-violent. There is no doubt that alcohol reduces inhibitions, which can of course be a good thing at a convivial social gathering, but problems arise from its use when a couple have problems with domestic violence.

The fights can become addictive

There is another, more insidious, factor in the causes of violence, and this is the fact that a couple may have a better and more fulfilling sexual experience after a fight. It probably has something to do with the fact that in the fight they are emotionally aroused, with physical contact too, and this acts for them as a kind of foreplay. The problem is that they may become addicted to it, and feel that it is the only good way to prepare for a satisfactory sexual experience. It can sometimes be romanticised as a legitimate kind of intimacy, and people feel that to 'kiss and make up' after a fight is a good way to manage a relationship.

CASE EXAMPLE

Eustace (41) and Elly (39) had been together for four years. Both had unconventional backgrounds, he describing himself as a 'down-and-out singer' and she having travelled widely and worked in various careers. She had two boys from an earlier relationship, aged fifteen and eleven. They lived together in Elly's house, and the couple's relationship was passionate and sexual, but sometimes violent. In fact, many of the arguments began with Eustace trying to discipline the boys, and Elly trying to restrain him. Their arguments would also often escalate to name-calling and threats to separate, and these could also end with a physical fight. Elly had needed to be taken to casualty twice with a suspected fracture of the arm. The couple were able in therapy to take joint responsibility for their arguments, to soften their voice tone during arguments and to avoid violence by speaking more slowly, and going to different rooms if an argument seemed to be getting out of hand. They also came to a better understanding of how to discuss discipline for the boys before taking unilateral action.

Why is the violence tolerated?

In some couples the violence can be very frequent. Women are more often the victims of the severe attacks, and there may be many incidents of bruising, visits to accident and emergency departments, and a significant fear of serious injury or death before they decide to do anything about it. Why do so many women put up with violence? Probably it has to do with the sincerity of their reconciliations after the incidents, and the love that they still feel for their partner in spite of the attacks. It may sometimes also be a question of fear of their partner stalking them if they do separate. For many women in this situation, the continuation of their relationship seems to be more important to them than their own personal safety. The male partners, on the other hand, do not see the violence as a major problem. They may sometimes blame their partner for the problem, citing 'provocation'. They may also feel that the degree of violence has been exaggerated by their partner, and they will often have an unrealistic hope that they can keep the problem under control.

The children may become involved

Children may become involved in the fights either as victims or in attempting to come between their fighting parents. It is not unusual for children to be injured in the process, sometimes directly by one or other parent, or more likely accidentally when an object is thrown. This may make it more obvious to the parents that something needs to be done about the problem, but it may take some time, and there may be several injuries to a child before they take action to reduce the violence. It is also well known that children who are brought up in a violent household are more likely to resort to violence themselves when in an adult relationship.

How to reduce the violence: take responsibility, negotiate and communicate

There is usually a whole sequence of events leading to a violent episode, and the sequence can be interrupted at any point. The stages may be:

- A difference of opinion
- An argument
- Provocation
- Raised voices
- Name-calling
- Pushing

- Throwing objects
- Hitting
- Kicking
- All leading to a risk of more serious injury

It is best to try to interrupt this sequence in the earlier stages, so that the risk of violence is less. The suggestions here therefore focus on tackling it at the beginning of the process, and we will begin at the point of first contact.

Take responsibility for your own actions

When you resort to violence it is never someone else's responsibility. We have on many occasions heard the words *'She drove me to it by her shouting'*, or *'I was only trying to restrain her'*. These excuses can never justify violence, and if an argument is getting dangerous you should always leave the area, perhaps immediately going out of the house or to a different room.

Avoid alcohol when you are together

This may seem like a 'killjoy' piece of advice, but the dangers of alcohol in provoking violence are well established, and if you have had violent episodes in the past it may be that alcohol is just too risky for you when you are together. This includes of course drinking when you are on your way home, and includes both partners, because the partner who becomes the victim of violence may be disinhibited by alcohol as much as the perpetrator. Unfortunately, we also have to add the caution that drinking a small 'agreed' amount of alcohol is a poor idea, because of the notorious problem that one drink leads to another. So, no alcohol is the only safe option (see Chapter 8).

Solve your differences by negotiation

This takes us right back to the exercises we recommended in Chapter 5. It is vital before you start negotiating to 'call a truce', as described there. This means no arguing and no violence for the duration of your discussions. As we suggested in Chapter 5, you should sit down together and put a timer on. You should then state the complaints that you have, convert them into requests for the other person to do things differently, set tasks for each other on a more-or-less equal basis, and then try to put the new regime into action over the next period of time. You should then move away from each other at the end of the time for a few minutes apart, before getting on with your daily routine. The process of negotiation is not guaranteed to prevent violence, but may over a few weeks create a more peaceful atmosphere. There may be a problem with keeping the peace while you are negotiating, and you may then use some of the methods for avoiding violence explained later in this chapter, or you may ask a trusted friend or relative to be with you in the negotiating sessions to keep the peace.

Communication can be improved

Again referring back to Chapter 5, you can learn to communicate more effectively. The most important thing to control is the way you address each other. You are probably in the habit of speaking quite quickly and quite loudly, and in the communication exercise we would ask you to speak more slowly, to use a quiet tone of voice and to make sure that you give plenty of time for the other person to reply before you start again. As we said in Chapter 5, the only person you can really change is yourself, and if you want the other partner to change it will be most effectively achieved by you making a change first. Rather than accusing them of speaking too loudly you should lower your own voice and try to help them to do so by example. Rather than saying to them that they are interrupting you, try to make sure you leave gaps in what you yourself are saying and reply slowly and carefully to what they say. Make sure that you look at your partner when they are speaking, and if possible when you are speaking to them. Try to be aware of when you are being provocative: sometimes you can say the same things in a much quieter and more peaceful way without changing the sense.

The pillow game

If it is difficult to slow down your discussion together, you could try holding a pillow or cushion while you speak and passing it over to your partner when they are speaking. The 'rule' would be that the person holding the pillow is the only one who can speak, and the other person is not allowed to take it from them. However, you will probably also need to make a further rule that no one speaks for more than thirty seconds without handing over the pillow.

Other rules of communication

As in Chapter 5, you should if possible always start your sentences with 'I' rather than 'you'. You should also try to make it possible for your partner to take up what you are saying in a constructive way. For example, rather than saying *'You are always aggressive to me'*, you could say *'I really like it when you are gentle and loving, and I hope you will be that way more often'*. In a similar way, you should try to end on a positive note. For example, rather than saying *'You have been a bit better this week, but why couldn't you have done this earlier'*, you could try saying *'I've waited quite a long time for this, but it's good that you have been a bit better this week'*. You will find that your partner will respond more positively to the second form of words, because the positive bit, instead of being put first, was said at the end.

Settling arguments

Going now to Chapter 6, you can use the 'arguments' exercise, although we would not suggest that you deliberately start arguments. We are using the exercise as a way of settling the arguments that arise spontaneously. You will certainly get into arguments in these communication sessions, even if you are trying to avoid them, and it will help if you can use some strategies for settling the arguments.

- The first rule is never to let the argument become so fierce that you begin to resort to violence. If there is a danger of this, you should stop right away and move into different rooms.
- If the argument is becoming childish, such as a *'yes it is'*, *'no it isn't'* type of argument, you might try to retrieve the situation by stopping, returning to the beginning and starting again. The difficulty is, however, that you may already have resorted to name-calling, and that is the stage before pushing and shoving.
- If pushing and shoving happens, you should treat the situation seriously, stop the discussion and move to separate rooms.

Agree to differ

Ideally, as we said in Chapter 6, an argument should have no winners or losers, and if you cannot agree on the issues you are discussing, you should try to 'agree to differ', in other words to accept that you have differing opinions and respect each other's right to disagree. This means that the argument has not been solved, but you may then decide to get some more information before the next discussion, to think about your position and maybe soften it, or to come around to your partner's point of view. In the calm of a break from argument, it is sometimes easier to move from an entrenched position and compromise.

If the violence has already begun: use avoidance tactics

If you have already got into a violent confrontation, even if it is only one of you who is being violent, you have both got a number of tactics you can use to reduce the violence.

- You can deliberately speak more quietly.
- You can leave a longer time before you reply *('I need time to think')*.
- You can discuss the fact that the violence has begun and that you need to stop it getting any worse.
- You can move away from each other physically, either to somewhere further apart in the same room or to different rooms.
- If you feel very angry and want to say something negative, try counting up to twenty before you speak (and then say it more gently).
- Whatever happens, if there are children in the house you should keep them away from the violent confrontation.

- The more violent partner (usually the man) may seek anger management therapy, which gives him techniques to avoid his uncontrollable rages (see Useful addresses).
- If the worst happens and there is actual violence, one of you should leave the house, preferably the one who has been violent, but if necessary the other one, taking the children with you if necessary.

Many couples who have violent disputes and physical fights have been able to improve their relationship to the point that they can stay together safely by using these fairly simple rules of conduct. The turning point is often when both partners realise that they must cooperate in order to do something about the problem. Instead of fighting over every issue, with one partner having to win, they agree to share the responsibility and the blame for their problems. It has been suggested that they might make a 'non-violent' contract, in which both partners agree that they will not resort to violence for a designated period, and this can be extended to longer periods as they manage to live without violence.

What if you cannot control the violence?

In this case the couple must agree to separate. It is not always possible to do this without further disputes. Often a woman who has been violently assaulted may be reluctant to take decisive action against her partner, partly because she is afraid of the consequences (perhaps further violence and threats of harm) and partly because she is motivated by love for him, and wants to believe that he can reform. When, however, the woman does agree that separation is imperative, there may be a further problem in getting her partner's cooperation. In the worst cases the man may refuse to give up his partner and family, even if there is a risk of serious harm or even death if the violence continues. Probably he will refuse to leave the family home himself. He will also resist any attempt by his partner and children to leave, making threats to anyone who tries to protect his partner. In these sort of situations there is no alternative but to get the help of the police (call 999 in an emergency or contact the local Community Safety Unit) or social services, and for the woman to leave home. It may be best, if there is a threat of further violence, to use a women's refuge, at an address that is kept secret from all except the workers and the women and children involved. This is to prevent the man from turning up there, stalking the partner and threatening her and the children. Information about refuges in the UK can be found through the organisation Women's Aid (see Useful addresses).

The use of a refuge is designed as a short-term solution to the problem of the uncooperative man with a history of battering. Usually with the help of legal aid it is possible for the woman to take out an injunction against the man, prohibiting him from coming near her place of residence. However, it often seems to extend into weeks or months before there can be an effective legal framework in place to protect the woman and her children from a violent partner. Thus the refuge remains a very important safeguard for those women who, following a series of episodes in which violence has been used, make the painful decision to separate against their partner's wishes.

Key Points

- Domestic violence arises from many sources, including male domination, but in many cases it can be the accidental outcome of an argument.
- It can be dangerous, and sometimes fatal.
- Factors that make it more likely are alcohol, an insistence on winning arguments and the excitement that it provides.
- Women sometimes tolerate extreme violence out of love, loyalty or fear of their partners.
- Suggestions are made in this chapter as to how to interrupt the 'escalation' process between a simple argument and severe violence.
- Advice is given on negotiation, communication and the avoidance of alcohol.
- Solving arguments in a friendly way by 'agreeing to differ' can reduce violence.
- If you really have to separate, it may be necessary to use a women's refuge.

10

Divorce and separation

Introduction

As we pointed out in Chapter 1, the divorce rate in most of the Western world has reached a very high level, and shows no sign of decreasing. This is not a disaster in itself, because many marriages involve painful levels of conflict, and for many, including the children involved, the most humane solution is divorce. Indeed, not all relationships can, or should, last 'till death us do part'. But when divorce happens there are severe consequences for the individuals involved, both adults and children. A divorce is like a bereavement, and in some cases it feels worse than a bereavement through death, because your ex-partner is still around but no longer wants to be with you. It leaves the ex-partners more vulnerable to various diseases, including cancer, heart disease and alcohol abuse (see Chapter 1). The general opinion among researchers is that divorced men are probably more at risk of physical illness than divorced women in the aftermath of the split, although divorced women are more likely to suffer from depression. A recent study identified that the presence of any of eighteen different mental disorders were positively associated with divorce, especially the presence of depression, alcohol abuse and specific phobias. Children of divorced parents are also more likely to be disadvantaged educationally and in their psychological adjustment than those whose parents are together. Added to this are the statistics that show that second marriages are, if anything, less stable than first marriages, and more likely to end in divorce. Thus the idea of 'getting it right the second time' is not as realistic as it might seem to the divorcing couple.

Divorce is not always an easy process. There are three main steps to getting divorced. These are:

1. You must file a divorce petition.
2. If your spouse agrees to the petition, you'll get a document saying you can apply for a decree nisi.
3. You need to wait at least six weeks after the date of the decree nisi before you can apply for a decree absolute that legally ends your marriage. You can remarry when you have the decree absolute.

You are able to arrange your own divorce without involving solicitors. If you both agree that your marriage has permanently broken down then you will not have to go to a court hearing. The court will deal with your divorce based on the submitted paperwork that is fairly straightforward if you both agree on the reasons for the divorce.

The divorce petition can only be submitted if the marriage has been in place for a year. One of five reasons must be established for the marriage to be deemed to have irrevocably broken down. These are adultery, unreasonable behaviour (this could include physical violence, verbal abuse including insults or threats, drunkenness or taking drugs or refusing to pay for housekeeping), desertion of two years, or separation for two years (if divorce is agreed) or five years (if divorce is contested). In Chapter 9 we considered the many ways that domestic abuse can impact on a relationship, and as 'unreasonable behaviour' is the commonest cause cited for filing a divorce petition, we suggest reading through Chapter 9 again if one or both of you want to try to keep the relationship together.

A recent study found that filings for divorce consistently peaked in March and August, the periods following winter and summer holidays. The conclusions were that troubled couples may see the holidays as a time to mend relationships over Christmas time or the summer holiday but disillusionment follows when unhappy spouses find that the holidays do not live up to expectations.

Unmarried couples are often called cohabitants or 'common-law husband and wife'. Of course, this can also be the agreement for some same-sex couples. The legal rights are different to those couples who are married and this can often lead to further disagreements during a time of separation, and can be challenging when there are children involved.

For same-sex couples in a Civil Partnership or Marriage, the process for dissolution is the same as for divorce. The

exception is adultery that is specific for heterosexual relationships ('sexual intercourse with someone of the opposite
sex outside marriage') although unreasonable behaviour can
be cited as the reason for the dissolution.

Divorce and separation as a last resort

It follows that it would be preferable, as far as possible, to
avoid the risk of a relationship ending, especially if there are
children involved. However, this does not mean that a marriage must be kept from breaking up at all costs, and there
are certainly some couples who are much better off apart
than together. The message from the earlier chapters in this
book is that there are many different ways of improving a
relationship, and that if they can be deployed then maybe
some divorces can be postponed or prevented. Examples are
the planned and timed discussions mentioned in Chapter 5,
the trivial arguments and timetables from Chapter 6, and
the ways of negotiating the differences between you on
sexual issues as outlined in Chapter 7.

It is our opinion that divorce should be seen as a last
resort, when all else has failed. This is partly because the
stability of marriage (or similar relationships) is worth maintaining if it can be achieved, and partly because the aftermath of divorce is difficult to predict and is complicated
both for the couple and for any children involved. One
way of moving away from the inevitability of a divorce is
to consider whether the personal issues that are driving you
towards divorce are more or less important than the stability

of the relationship. The next three sections will help you to think about how you might look at alternatives.

You can't insist on your partner staying with you, but you can insist on divorcing

Divorce, if it has to happen, should be a bilateral decision, with both of you deciding that it is the only possible course, and that the separation is the least bad solution to your problems. Usually, however, there is one partner who is keener on it than the other. Often this is in the context of an affair involving that partner, and they want to form a new relationship and therefore separate. In other cases one partner makes the decision that they can no longer put up with the behaviour of the other one, or they have 'fallen out of love' and must separate. Here the power is in the hands of the partner who has made the decision that the relationship is at an end, and the other partner cannot insist on staying together. Putting this another way, it takes two people to decide to stay together, but either of them can decide on their own to go ahead with the divorce.

Think about it carefully and weigh the pros and cons

When you get to the point of thinking about divorce, it is helpful to consider carefully what is about to happen, and to make a list of the advantages and disadvantages of staying together against the advantages and disadvantages of divorcing. These might be of various sorts, and at different timescales: for example, you might consider the situation in five years' time, and look at what this would be like (a) if a divorce had gone ahead or (b) if you had stayed together. To take a common example of this, if the husband in a marriage with two children has been having an affair with a younger woman, and wants to separate and live with her, you might consider the advantages and disadvantages as follows:

Advantages of Divorce

- Husband goes with the woman he wants to be with
- Husband loses the stress of living a double life
- Wife can live more peacefully without the stress of the conflict
- Wife can plan her own life, and possibly form a new relationship
- Good for the husband's girlfriend, who wants to be with him

Disadvantages of Divorce

- Expense of the legal case
- Both partners poorer as a result of the divorce
- Risk of a bitter conflict following the divorce

- Problems of moving and getting two separate places
- Wife could become depressed
- Husband could feel guilty
- Problems with care of children, including disputes over payments and access
- Both partners may have further children, maybe disadvantaging their own children (see Chapter 11)

Advantages of Staying Together

- Less expensive for both
- More stability for children
- Couple remain in the family home
- Living through a 'bad patch' might strengthen the relationship

Disadvantages of Staying Together

- Conflict may continue
- Wife may still be bitter and blame him
- Husband may continue his outside relationship
- If he gives it up he may be resentful

> • Wife may be reluctant to resume sexual relations
> • It may only be a short-term solution

Looking at the pros and cons

The above is one example of the kinds of consideration which couples need to take into account when they are wondering whether to divorce or not. There will in most cases be many other issues to be resolved, and many other pressures on the couple. For example, the husband's friends could bring pressure on him to divorce, perhaps because they themselves are now single and want him to lead a singles' life with them. The wife's family may have disapproved of the husband from the beginning, and prefer her to be away from him.

How can divorce or separation be avoided?

Once the threat of separation has been made by one partner, there is an immediate change in the situation. The partner who wants to stay together is not in a position to insist on staying together, and there may be a mountain to climb in persuading the other partner to reconcile. The couple may have been carrying on with their lives up to this point under the assumption that the relationship will continue whatever happens, and there may be some difficulty in accepting the new playing field.

Both must agree on trying to save the relationship

It takes two to work on improving a relationship, and you must both be willing at least to put the question of divorce aside for the period when you are working on the relationship. In the situation of a threatened divorce, it is that much more difficult for you to cooperate on couple communication and negotiation exercises, and it takes a great degree of goodwill to 'do-it-yourself' in these circumstances. You might be wise, as an alternative, to consider going to couple therapy, couple counselling or mediation (see below), when the therapist or mediator can contain some of the 'awfulness' for you, while working together with you both on reconciliation.

How would you go about trying to avoid divorce?

The exercises described in Chapters 5, 6 and 7 will be just as valid in the situation of a threat of divorce as they are in 'normal' relationship problems, but they may have to be carried out with more care and caution than usual because of the 'nuclear threat' hanging over you. For example, you might try setting a time for sitting together and talking, with a timer going, and discuss the reasons why one of you has come to this conclusion. The questions might focus on the practical aspects of what you might both have done to contribute to the problem. In your discussions, as in the regular exercises from earlier chapters, you will need to concentrate as far as possible on the positives, and try to convert your complaints into requests of each other for improvements in behaviour. This leaves your partner the chance to make a concession or positive response rather than 'stonewalling'.

The need for moderate language and behaviour

If you are trying to save the relationship, it would be better for you to avoid as far as possible the extreme language and adversarial attitudes that one often reads of in the divorce courts.

- Words such as 'unreasonable' and 'impossible' are best not used, while you should concentrate on a milder use of language, such as 'irritating' or 'hard to accept'.
- Perhaps there has been violence between you: this should be talked about as 'our fights' rather than 'your tantrums' or 'your aggression'.
- Similarly, complaints about alcohol abuse, gambling, lying and overspending will have to be softened in order to get both of you talking constructively about the issues.
- Remember to talk as far as possible in the 'I' mode rather than starting with 'you' (see Chapter 5).

In order to put your relationship back on course, you must both make more of an effort to change your own behaviour, leading to cooperation rather than confrontation. You will probably have a natural wish to punish your partner for what you feel they have done, but even if they admit it all, and apologise, their sense of humiliation may lead them either to show increased hostility or somehow to sabotage the process. It is still better to soft-pedal at this stage.

What if one partner has been unfaithful?

This is a common situation, and one of the most frequent grounds for divorce. If the couple are to continue in their relationship, perhaps mainly for the sake of the children, there has to be some way in which the other partner can accept and even forgive the partner who has had the affair. Forgiveness may require three processes:

- Recognising the impact of the traumatic event
- Understanding the meaning it has for both partners
- Moving on and rebuilding the couple's life together

This is often very hard to do, especially if it has involved lies and covering up, perhaps by mutual friends as well as by the partner. One way to achieve this difficult task is for the wronged partner to accept that their relationship can never be quite as trusting and intimate as it had been before the affair, and that, although disappointing, perhaps this is a more realistic way to treat it. The previous trust could be said to have been misplaced, and in the new situation the couple could be said to be taking a 'wiser' and more realistic attitude to their relationship than before. They can still enjoy each other's company, and still have a rewarding interaction with their children, despite the affair having occurred. In some couples there is even a more exciting sexual life after the affair, because of the fact of one partner having fulfilled their sexual fantasy and being seen as a more interesting lover for that reason.

CASE EXAMPLE

Marion and Charles, in their forties, almost reached breaking point in their relationship because Marion had had an affair. The affair was with a man she met on holiday, and was not likely to meet again without a lot of difficulty. The problem was that she and Charles had a rather unexciting sex life, and it was obvious to him that sex in the affair had been more exciting for her. They worked hard on reconciling, partly because they wanted to avoid hurting their two children, and the extended families were also in favour of them continuing together if possible. Their therapy was partly directed to finding a way for Charles to think more positively about Marion, and treating her as someone whom he could respect again. It also concentrated on helping them to find a more satisfying sex life, and in particular to help Charles with his problem of premature ejaculation (see Chapter 7). They have stayed together and now have a more satisfying and rewarding general and sexual relationship than before the affair.

What if there has been an 'irretrievable breakdown'?

This implies more than the 'unreasonable behaviour' of the earlier paragraph, in that both partners seem to agree that the situation has gone beyond their powers of recovery. We would still believe that it is worth examining the situation to see whether some reconciliation is possible, and a couple who have come to this conclusion may still have the possibility of getting together with a therapist or mediator and working on the relationship. They would probably first have to agree to look at the pros and cons of divorce (see above) and then decide whether it is inevitable that a divorce will go ahead or whether there is some hope of reconciliation.

Ways to have a better divorce

If you decide that divorce is inevitable, you may find that the process is both painful and expensive. Even when you and your partner have agreed that you both want to divorce, and you have both agreed that you want to make the best arrangement for the family as a whole, there will still be legal ends that have to be tied up, and this will cost money. However, if you are into an acrimonious divorce, with mistrust on both sides and perhaps only communicating through lawyers, the process becomes much more complicated and expensive. It may seem to you that all you want is to get the best solution for you both, but the likelihood is that your partner will oppose you, and what seems fair and honest to you may seem totally one-sided to your partner. In the situation of divorce, opposition is expensive, because the lawyers you employ have the sole aim of getting the best result for you, their client, while the lawyers on the other side want to get the best result for your partner. If it goes to court the result can be that the legal process costs more than either of you have to share between you.

The possibilities of mediation

If you have decided to divorce, separate or to dissolve your civil partnership, it is possible to consider family mediation to help make and agree future arrangements for your children, property and finances. This is a voluntary process. By avoiding court and lawyers, it can lead to quicker settlement with less conflict and stress for both of you. You also get to stay in control of the arrangements rather than handing it over to the courts. There are a number of different providers of mediation and it is worth choosing carefully, in a way similar to choosing a solicitor or other professional.

Mediation may not be necessary in a divorce in which both sides are agreed on a mutually fair distribution of their wealth, and agree on the care of children. However, this is rarely the case, and in most divorces there is the possibility that mediation can help. It is particularly valuable in terms of the couple's continued responsibility for 'co-parenting' their children after a separation.

What Is Mediation About?

- It is a process whereby the couple voluntarily engage in discussions with a neutral third party to reach proposals for settlement of issues, mostly to do with money, property and the care of children, which they can then have endorsed by their own legal representatives.
- Mediation can be 'child-centred' or 'comprehensive' (also called 'All Issues Mediation').
- Child-centred mediation is usually done by family therapists or counsellors, and is mainly concerned with residence of the children and arrangements for visiting.
- Comprehensive mediation deals with all issues, including financial, childcare and housing, and is usually done by either a team including counsellors and lawyers, or by individuals with training in both legal and counselling matters.

In either type of mediation the couple may be seen together or separately, and in many settings the children are seen, either alone or with their parents. Stages in the process include:

- Establishing the forum (including the decision whether to involve the children).
- Clarifying the issues and setting the agenda.
- Exploring the issues.
- Developing the options.
- Securing agreement (to be taken to the lawyers for ratification).

Mediation can be very successful, but this depends on the level of cooperation the mediators can get from the couple. It is generally seen as a cheaper option than leaving it all to the lawyers. More importantly, couples who go through mediation tend to feel that they have had a more amicable divorce than couples who simply use lawyers. They also tend to have more trouble-free childcare arrangements. It has been found, however, that very conflicted couples are often unable to make use of mediation, because they do not have the basic level of cooperation to begin the process.

Children: how do they react to the split?

One of the enduring problems arising from divorce is the effect that it has on any children within the relationship. As we mentioned earlier, they can be disadvantaged both educationally and psychologically by divorce, but there are also more specific problems encountered as they go through the split-up of their parents. These problems differ according to the age of the children at the time of the split.

* Very young children (under four years old) find it difficult to understand the motives of other people, and often assume that it is their fault if Mummy or Daddy has gone away.
* Up to the age of seven they still find the changes hard to understand, but may be able to empathise with one parent at a time, and can enjoy the time they spend with both.
* From seven to nine there is an increasing ability to comprehend mixed feelings, and to accept the changes in their family life.
* In late childhood (age nine to thirteen) they may express clear preferences between parents, but not want to hurt the rejected parent.
* In adolescence they may begin to take sides more openly, but may also try to be the peacemaker. Boys are more likely to show problem behaviour, while girls are more likely to become depressed.

At any age, the children may show increased difficulties in behaviour. These are usually more severe if there is conflict between the parents, and often pre-date the divorce. The worst scenario for the children is when there is severe conflict between the parents before and after the divorce. In the process the children are asked to take sides by one or both parents, and they may even be used as pawns in the power struggle that is going on. The best that a parental couple who are splitting can do is to work together as far as possible to maintain their children's peace of mind.

What might make it easier for the children?

There are many children whose parents have divorced, as well as many others who have always been in a one-parent family. The fact that this is now a common situation makes it easier for the children whose parents are divorcing to accept it, partly because it appears more usual than an exception. School friends whose parents may also have divorced can also be a help in coming to terms with the breakup. Teachers too may be a resource, and it is always useful for the class teacher to be informed of the split, so that the child can be given support in school. Grandparents will often wish to help with childcare, as well as being someone the child can confide in.

How to tell the children

The first priority is to tell the children what is happening. What you tell them will vary according to how old they are.

If they are very young, it would be best to make it very simple, but always to bear in mind the risk that they may take it personally and think that they are somehow at fault. With the younger children the message will have to be repeated, perhaps many times, to ensure that they have absorbed it. If they are older, then they should be given more details about what is happening, and in an ideal world it would be better if they heard it from both parents together. This may not be possible, however, if the two parents can't cooperate to this extent, and the next best arrangement is for both of you to speak to them separately, having had a prior discussion together and then each saying more or less the same thing. It is essential that your children are not blamed for the split, and that they are reassured that you both love them and wish to care for them.

You are still co-parents to your children

The fact that they must remain good co-parents is almost a golden rule for the divorcing parental couple. The children should not have to make decisions about their own care, although their views should be taken into account when decisions are made. Being 'co-parents', even though you may not be living together, means sharing responsibility for the welfare of your children, even though in the case of a non-resident parent that will be delegated to the resident parent. It also means making joint decisions on their behalf when necessary (mainly when the children are younger) and taking the children's views into consideration when they are old enough to be consulted.

The parental child

When a parent who is divorced lives with their children, one of the children may become part of the 'parental system', a so-called parental child. They may take a role of replacement partner to the lone parent, and take too great a level of responsibility for the care of younger siblings. This may be a safe course for a short time, but if it continues for long it will cause developmental problems for the child. If you see this situation developing, you should try to talk it out with the parental child, take back some of the decision making and responsibility, and help the child to resume their role as an ordinary family member. This means that, if they have their own problems, they can once again come to you as their parent, rather than supporting you all the time.

Problems of access where the parents live a long way from each other

It is much better for divorcing parents, if possible, to find accommodation within reasonable travelling distance from each other. Particular problems arise when the divorcing parents choose to live in different countries, or even different continents. The further the distances, the harder it is to arrange regular contact between the children and the non-resident parent. In a poll of four thousand parents twenty years after the 1989 Children Act, it was found that a third of all non-resident fathers have lost contact with their children after separation, regardless of where they live, and this proportion is higher if there are long distances involved. It is important to try to keep contact going by telephone, letter and by use of social media as well as internet technologies like FaceTime and email, and even where they live far away this can be a good way to maintain relationships with absent children. It is sobering to read that a third of children from broken families in the poll mentioned had been tempted by alcohol or drugs and one in ten later become involved in crime.

What if the children get upset after a visit?

This is not at all unusual (see Chapter 11 for further discussion) for all sorts of reasons. There may be tensions between you and your ex-partner which are being played out through the children, or they may just be upset at the change of routine, or at the reminder that you are no longer together. It would be very tempting for either partner to decide as a result that it would be better to stop visits. This would be a mistake, and may lead to further problems in the children's future adjustment. It is better to persevere with visiting, however difficult to arrange and potentially upsetting, rather than risk the absent parent losing contact.

What about the grandparents?

Although your partner becomes your ex-partner following a divorce or separation, you don't become ex-parents, and your own parents don't become ex-grandparents. They still have a valid claim to continue their relationship with your children, and it is up to you to help them to maintain that relationship if that is what both they and your children want. In fact, grandparents may become an essential link in the chain, if perhaps there is a problem with the non-resident parent meeting with the children, either due to a lack of a suitable place or because the resident parent objects to the other one seeing the children alone. In any case, the grandparent will usually want to send presents, attend school events, and support the child in other activities. There may be specific difficulties regarding Christmas, weddings and similar occasions, when the grandparents will often want to get together with their grandchildren in spite of the divorce, and see a chance of some kind of family solidarity at least on a temporary basis. The secret of arranging these occasions is to avoid too much contact between the two partners, especially if there is a lot of ongoing conflict.

What if you go on to have new relationships?

It may be a great relief for the divorcing couple that life does not have to be lived as a single parent forever, but a new relationship brings its own sources of conflict and confusion for the partners themselves and for the children and other relatives. There are often divided loyalties in this situation, and there are many other difficulties to be surmounted by the ex-partners getting into new relationships. The most important thing is to keep your ex-partner and the children informed as soon as the new relationship becomes permanent. These issues are dealt with in the next chapter, which in many ways could be seen as a continuation of this one.

Key Points

- Divorce should be a last resort.
- Although it is often a relief, it can be like a bereavement.
- Divorce can be entirely orchestrated by one partner, but it takes two to agree to attempt reconciliation.
- You should carefully weigh the pros and cons of divorce as against staying together.
- In avoiding divorce you could use the techniques from earlier chapters, such as negotiation, communication (avoiding extreme language), solving arguments and using timetables.
- You may have to consider forgiveness for infidelity by one partner.
- If divorce is inevitable, mediation can help to resolve the disputes.
- The welfare of your children is paramount: try not to move too far away, arrange regular visiting and remain good co-parents.
- Remember the grandparents, who will not want to lose touch with their grandchildren.
- If you get into new relationships, keep everyone informed.

11

Blended families (stepfamilies)

Introduction

There is an increasing number of second marriages, and an even larger number of people who are divorced and getting together in cohabiting relationships. The question is, what happens to the children in these families? In many cases they will be living at different times with parents who may both be in new relationships. We will be using the term 'blended family' for a family with step-parents, stepchildren or more informal arrangements in which children live with their parents' new partners who are not related to them. We will also be using the terms 'stepfather' and 'stepmother' for new partners of the divorcing parents even if they are not married to them.

Although we have used the heterosexual model as the norm in this chapter, the issues are very similar to those occurring in the increasing number of same-sex relationships which include children, either biological or adopted. There are very few aspects of the advice given which are not common to both situations.

The negative image of step-parents, in contrast to the idealisation of the new relationship

A large number of folk tales involve wicked stepmothers (for example *Cinderella* and *Snow White*), and an equal number of stories feature stepfathers who are cruel or sexually abusive. Another common situation in literature and the media is the rivalry that may exist between a girl and her new stepmother for the affections of her father, and the sexual feelings that a boy may experience for his father's (often younger) partner. These situations do indeed sometimes arise: they are not just myths.

In total contrast to these negative images is the optimistic belief some new couples have that, because of the strength of their feelings for each other, their children will get along well with them both, and the new family will be free of trouble. Neither the negative view of literature nor the over-optimistic hopes of the new couple are really representative of the situation that usually exists when a blended family is created. There are often problems, but they can usually be solved with goodwill on all sides.

Problems for the couple themselves

For people who are starting out on a relationship following a divorce or a separation from a previous partner, even if there are no children involved, there are complex issues. There may be resentment against the previous partner, which can sour the present relationship. There may be guilt about leaving the marriage, which can lead to an apparent lack of commitment to the present partner. There is also the problem of idealisation, in that those who enter a new relationship are often trying to heal the wounds of the previous breakup in their optimism about the success of the new relationship.

The necessity for realism

Second relationships are usually more difficult than first ones. The couple are admittedly older and more experienced than when they married the first time, but they may also have lost some of the enthusiasm that they brought to the earlier relationships. It is tempting to paint the ex-partner as all bad and the new partner as all good, and this can often sustain the couple for a while. However, this is a risky strategy, because the new partner then has a lot to live up to, and there is bound to be a problem sooner or later. It takes just as long for a new relationship to develop as for the original one, and these things cannot be hurried. It is also helpful not to have unrealistic sexual expectations in a second relationship, especially if the man is over fifty. Sometimes the couple are disappointed that their 'honeymoon' is not as good sexually as they had hoped, but this can usually be dealt with by having a sympathetic discussion about the natural changes of middle age (see Chapter 3).

What about the daily routines of living?

When a couple begin to live together after one or both

have broken up with previous partners, there are a host of everyday habits and routines which need to be adjusted. With a bit of discussion and negotiation (see Chapter 5) it can usually be resolved between you, and the question of clothes on the bedroom floor and leaving the toothpaste tube open does not have to destroy the new relationship as soon as it is formed.

Setting up a blended family

If there are children from the earlier relationships, then sooner or later the new couple will have to set up a full-time or part-time blended family. Usually the mother of the children will be the main carer for them. This means that families with a resident stepfather are more likely to involve children being there all or most of the time. In 'stepmother' families, the more common pattern is for alternate week-ends with the children, along with extra contact at holiday times. These are by no means universal arrangements, and many variations are possible, including shared care arrangements with each parent having the children 50 per cent of the time. Whether looking after children full-time or part-time, the couple will have many of the same issues to face.

Try if possible not to live too far away from each other

Divorcing couples will have problems with children visiting if they live a long way from each other, the most extreme situation being if they live on different continents. In planning your life with a new partner, it makes sense to think of children's visiting arrangements and to work out a sensible way of organising the travel at weekends. If it really is not possible to live nearby, longer but less frequent visits might be able to be arranged, with a fair degree of reliability and predictability.

Keep ex-partners and children informed of any changes

If you have been seeing someone regularly and decide to live together or get married, it is always wise to tell your ex-partner and your children as soon as possible what is happening, especially if there is to be a visit. It can be upsetting for the children to meet their new stepmother or stepfather without having been warned about it. The same applies to moving, arrangements for school and plans for holidays. It may not always be easy for couples who have had an acrimonious divorce to communicate about practical issues, and sometimes an intermediary may have to be brought in, for example one of the grandparents or a trusted mutual friend, to pass on the information.

The new relationship and the ages of the children

Children under five usually find it easier than older children to adjust to step-parents. The older children may have a secret idea that the new relationship will not last and that their biological parents will get together again. They may well also have heard their mother or father talking in negative terms about the other parent's new partner, and perhaps feel that they would be disloyal to accept the new relationship. The introductions between the children and the new partner are crucial, in that they can set the pattern of future meetings and interactions.

The roles that children have had before, and their new roles

Often when a mother is divorced, one of the older children becomes her confidant, and takes a somewhat parental role. This can seem at the time to be good for the child's self-esteem, and can help with the stress caused by the split. However, the 'parental' role for a child is risky (see Chapter 10) and can interfere with the child's natural development. It should only be allowed on a very limited and temporary basis, to overcome a crisis. In any case, when a new partner comes to live with the family, there is usually an expectation that the child will revert to being a child again, and this may be problematic, with hostility to the step-parent. One way to manage this is to give the parental child a special role in the new stepfamily, such as (if they are old enough) looking after younger children from time to time.

The children's expectations may be very different from yours

The children's expectations are not always very positive, especially if the new relationship is formed soon after the separation. There is thus a sharp contrast between the children's attitudes and those of the new couple, who may be very enthusiastic about the new arrangements. The problem is that the new couple may be assuming that they can quickly create a successful 'nuclear' family with their children/stepchildren, and they could easily begin to blame the children for failing to adjust to the situation. The contrast between their view and that of the children might be seen as the children grieving for the old relationship and the new partners wanting to celebrate the new one. You should be very aware of this when introducing children to your new partner or letting them know about new living arrangements.

Attitudes of the two biological parents to each other and to the new relationships

You should remember that the ex-partner is still psychologically present in the other one's new relationship, and that the ex-partner will probably have some discussion of the new relationship with the children on their return from a visit. This means that it would be better for both biological parents to be careful not to say negative things about the other parent or about that person's new partner in front of the children. As with our suggestions for dealing with problems within an ongoing relationship (Chapter 6) you should always think of the long-term stability of your children rather than trying to win a battle over your ex-partner. Your collaborative relationship as co-parents will potentially go on until your children have reached adult life, and it will be of great benefit to them if they have two biological parents who can work together in caring for them.

Boundaries, rules and discipline

This is one of the hardest areas for the new couple setting up a blended family. Most of the daily activities in a nuclear family are done automatically without any thought: we simply fit in with the routines and habits of those we live with. When a new couple are getting together and setting up house, they are having to deal with the differences in their own previous routines (see above), and working out compromises to fit their new situation. Children who are familiar with their old routines may become irritable or withdrawn if they feel uncomfortable with the new arrangements. This may then lead to them having clashes, either with the new step-parent or with both the partners, and the children may be labelled 'disturbed'. In coping with this problem it is best for the new couple to take things slowly, to adapt to the children's needs and to move gradually to a compromise position which does not disadvantage either the step-parent or the children.

Who can impose discipline?

At first in a blended family the resident biological parent, whether mother or father, should be the main disciplinarian, hopefully in collaboration or at least in consultation with the non-resident biological parent. The step-parent should defer to their new partner wherever possible, and should never make far-reaching decisions involving the children without reference to the partner. As the new system evolves it may become clear that both partners are trusted by each other and by the children to enforce discipline and to make decisions. But in the last analysis, and for very important decisions, it should always be the biological parent, in discussion with the absent parent, who decides. In Chapter 2 we described the parental subsystem, which acts as the decider system for the children; and with blended families that subsystem has three or four members, rather than two, and they may not always see eye to eye. However, they should all be informed about important or far-reaching decisions.

Case example

Betty (36) and Mark (41) have been divorced for two years. Mark is a psychotherapist, and has formed a live-in relationship with Anne, a colleague. His and Betty's children have had very varied reactions to Mark's new relationship. Alan (14) refuses point blank to meet with Anne, in spite of pressure from both Mark and Betty. He also takes the role of 'father substitute' towards Tony and Rachel, his younger siblings. Tony (12) has been acting as a go-between, and stays regularly at Mark's home; but at the family home, he and Betty have constant arguments and fights, in which Mark (although absent) intervenes on Betty's side. Rachel (9) likes to keep both parents happy, but doesn't take sides. Therapy took the form of meetings with Mark and Betty, including the three children on two occasions. The main thrust was to emphasise that Alan should be allowed to make his own decisions as to whether to meet with Anne. Betty was encouraged to work out a schedule for the three children to help with household matters (thus taking on the parental role towards Alan as well as the others) and to praise Tony for his work in the house rather than scolding him when he didn't do it. Rachel was praised for being the peacemaker. In the end, Alan still didn't go to meet Anne, and he became more detached from Betty, but Tony became a much more cooperative member of Betty's family, and the crisis was resolved.

Generation boundaries

When the children first meet with the new partner, they may treat them as a friend of the family, and only gradually learn that they are soon to be their step-parent. The new partner may be younger than the parent they are living with, and it may be difficult, especially for older children, to accept them as a step-parent, because of the difficulty of respecting someone who is nearer to them in age.

Intimate situations

There are particular areas where the step-parent will have to tread carefully in relation to the children. This is especially important in view of concerns about child sexual abuse. Intimate situations such as bath time (with younger children), the children's bedtime and the children coming into the couple's bed may have to be dealt with cautiously by the step-parent, and the children should be asked for their agreement for their new step-parent to take part in these activities. The absent parent should also be kept informed. Even if there is no sexual attraction between the children and the step-parent, it is wise to avoid situations that could be misunderstood. At first the biological parent should be present in all these situations, and only gradually should the step-parent take them over when necessary, with the agreement of both the resident parent and the absent parent. The absent parent will certainly hear about the arrangements in the new household, and it is best for them to be given the information in advance rather than hearing it from the children afterwards.

Risk of sexual involvement with stepchildren

In particular, the position of the new stepfather is a vulnerable one, and the risk of sexual involvement with stepsons or stepdaughters is one which he should be aware of. This may happen without any premeditation on his part, and research suggests that it is easier for a man to get into this situation if he is living with children he has not brought up from babyhood. Even if there is no involvement as such, it is wise to avoid any situations in which he might be suspected of it, or in which there might be the chance of a false accusation being made by a discontented child. If, however, a child does make a specific complaint about sexual involvement with a step-parent, the resident parent must take it seriously and act on it through the local social services.

School and friendship issues for the children

Children who live with one parent and their new partner will sooner or later be in a position when they have to talk about the home situation in school and with friends. This causes less trauma and less stigma than it used to when divorce was uncommon. Often there are other children in the class whose parents are divorced, or who come from a single-parent household. The teacher may be aware of the difficulties faced by children in this situation, and can facilitate discussion in class, for example about how many sisters and brothers each child has, or the problems of weekend visiting. This can have the effect of reducing stigma and aids the children's adjustment to the new living arrangements.

Step-siblings

In many blended families there are siblings from both parents' sides, and sometimes these children are quite close in age. There may be an instant friendship between them, or an instant dislike, but in most cases it will take some time before there is a reasonable adjustment between step-siblings. If they are not in contact all the time, but only at visiting times, this may make the situation easier;

but when there is full-time contact, the problem can be a more chronic one, and lead to depression or maladjustment on either side. Another potential difficulty is sexual attraction between step-siblings, and although they are not biologically related, the fact that they are part of the same family makes it necessary to discourage such relationships if possible.

What happens when the new couple have babies of their own?

This can be a great joy to them, and hopefully also to their older children, but the risk of resentment and rivalry is probably greater in the blended family than in nuclear families when a new baby is born. Often the child from the earlier relationship feels displaced and loses self-esteem. The couple should be careful not to exclude the older child from their new 'nuclear' family, and to avoid discriminating against them in giving them poorer presents, in paying for their education or in buying clothes or toys. Many children of divorced parents feel the advent of the new baby very acutely, and may need extra time to talk with their biological parent to gain reassurance about the new situation.

Family holidays

This often becomes an issue during the long school holidays, and both biological parents should come to some agreement about their plans for holidays to include the children.

It might be best for the non-resident parent and partner to take the children away for the longer break, since they see less of them during term-time. However, this will vary from family to family, and the only important thing is to make clear and reliable arrangements, which are agreed to by both biological parents and are acceptable to the children.

Festivals, especially Christmas

These pose special problems for the blended family. There is a tendency for the children to wish for a family reconciliation at these times, and they probably hope that their biological parents will get together and plan a reunion. However, the new couple(s) will also wish to have a good family celebration for themselves at Christmas, and this may be in conflict with the children's wishes. Each family will have to make its own arrangements, and this may be different in different years and at different festivals. The most important consideration is that the children are able to enjoy the festival. The new couple should probably use other times, for example holidays, for their 'couple time' together.

Weddings and funerals

As opposed to Christmas and similar festivals, family weddings and funerals usually bring together both the ex-partners, their children and the new partners. There are often high levels of anxiety and tension around such gatherings.

CASE EXAMPLE

To take the hypothetical example of a daughter who has been living with her mother and stepfather and visiting her father and stepmother on a regular basis: she may want both her biological parents to sit together at her wedding reception, but does not want her stepmother or stepfather to be at the same table as her parents. There may have to be a good deal of discussion about the seating, but an informal arrangement without a 'top' table may solve some of the problems. There may have to be some moving around at different stages of the reception, and the bride's wishes may not be able to be met in full because of the tension between the various people involved. It might even be that one of the new partners has to miss the ceremony, but this would be unfortunate, and would lead to the likelihood of further problems in the future.

Similar considerations apply to funerals, but here the solemnity of the occasion can sometimes overcome the antagonism between the ex-partners and the other people involved in the blended families, and can lead to more understanding. Again, if there is too much tension it may be better for those who are nearest to the person who has died to go to the funeral without their present partners.

Older children leaving home

This is a transition phase in the life of a blended family just as in a nuclear family, and the issues are quite similar. The children decide when the time is right to leave home, perhaps when they get into their own intimate partnership, go to college or get a job away from home. The parents, whether in a blended family or not, may allow them to leave, or may oppose it, and relations between parents and children may continue well or badly. One point to be made about this new situation is that the children are now free to keep in touch with both sets of parents, or with neither, as they choose.

Worries about stepchildren who have left

Problems can still emerge, even after the children have left the blended family, with the step-parent resenting the time and money that his or her partner expends on the children of their previous marriage. There may be issues about wills and inheritance, with one partner worrying about how much of the other partner's assets are going to his or her children after death. This can be more difficult to sort out legally if the two are in a long-standing relationship without being married.

Conclusions

Given the fact that so many people are now living in blended families, it is surprising that more is not written about the problems and how to solve them. What we have done here is to produce a brief and very general guide to the problems of blended families and their possible solutions. However, each family is truly unique, and a solution to one family's problems may not be applicable to others. The most important thing to remember is the vulnerability of children in this setting, especially in the early stages. The best protection for them is to have two biological parents who, though they don't stay married, are still working together as co-parents, with the help of their new partners, for the welfare of their children.

Key Points

In forming and maintaining a blended family, these are some things to bear in mind:

- Try if possible not to live too far away from your ex-partner.
- Keep your ex-partner informed as soon as possible of any changes in your status.
- Make sure that you and your ex-partner work together to inform the children about where they are to live, with whom and when.
- Try not to undermine or criticise your ex-partner or their new partner in front of the children: be positive about them.
- Remember that the children may not be as enthusiastic as you are about your new partner.
- Respect the different needs of children of different ages.
- Sometimes children have had a parental role before the 'blending' and may regret the loss of this.

- Remember that your relationship with your partner is 'younger' than your children's ages.
- Try to be consistent as a couple about the house rules and discipline when the blended family is together.
- Respect boundaries, and don't expect full family intimacy (e.g. at bath times) until the family has been established for some time.
- Make good and reliable arrangements for school and family holidays.
- Be aware of the pressures that your children may experience at school following the 'blending' of the family.
- Be aware that the children may respond with depression or behavioural problems to the new family setup.
- Remember that the birth of children to the new partners can cause negative feelings in the older children in a blended family.
- Be aware of the tensions that can occur around festivals, weddings and funerals when different strands of the families meet.
- Think about wills and inheritance, and who you want to benefit after your death.

12

Establishing a relationship

Introduction

Be clear what it is you want as a part of your life

There are many single people around, and although some single people are longing for a steady relationship, many of them, in spite of contrary messages in the media, are quite content to be single. You may be a naturally independent person, who has no need of an ongoing relationship to be happy. On the other hand, you may prefer to have many casual partners rather than committing yourself to one, and this is quite a common situation for those in their teens and twenties. The bottom line here is what you as a person are wanting, rather than what the media, your family or your friends think you should be wanting.

You may have been in a relationship but be widowed or have separated from your partner as we discussed in Chapter 10. After the natural grieving process following a death or separation, it can still be difficult to establish a new relationship. Changes in society, people living longer and new technologies can all make it more difficult to find your way through the maze without resorting to wearing the 'I'm single again' t-shirt in the local coffee shop.

If you really want a relationship

If you decide that you want to get into a long-term relationship, for the first or subsequent time, with the possibility of having a family, you may just find it very difficult to make the early moves necessary to meet with and attract someone. Or it may be that, having got into a casual relationship, you are unable to move this into a more permanent one. For some, too, there are a number of psychological issues such as anxiety and a fear of intimacy, which may also go together with shame or low self-esteem, and any of these issues can inhibit your efforts to get into a relationship. Some of these issues may be as a result of having grown up gay in a homophobic environment. This chapter will hopefully help you if any of these are the problems you have.

How are you going to meet new people?

Probably the most reliable way to start a relationship is by getting to know someone in the context of work, leisure activities, studying together, religious meetings or involvement in voluntary service. The advantage of these situations is that you are under no great compulsion to form a relationship, and things can proceed at a comfortable pace, or maybe not develop if it doesn't seem right for you as a couple. Some of the ideas that we mentioned in Chapter 1 are relevant: sexual attraction, mutual interests, toleration, shared ideals, ability to compromise and feeling comfortable with intimacy. All of these help the couple to know that they will have the possibility of a successful long-term relationship. It also helps if there is some similarity between you, in the sense of being able to share the same jokes and the same sad feelings. But beware of the concept of 'falling in love'; it is marvellous if it happens, but it is the exception rather than the rule, and if it does happen it brings with it a number of expectations which may often be unrealistic and which can lead to great disappointment if they are not met (see Chapter 1).

If, however, you don't have the opportunities to meet new partners as mentioned above, you may find that you have a problem in finding someone with whom you can get into a relationship. A lot of single people find it hard, for reasons including lack of money, lack of time or living a solitary life, to meet the kinds of people that they could relate to intimately. As we said, it is usually better to meet people in a context in which there is no special expectation of forming a relationship there and then, for example a social event such as a party or a gathering. Failing this, you may think of using more formal ways of getting in touch with possible partners.

Dating agencies

Dating agencies have been doing this kind of work for decades, following on from the work of marriage brokers and matchmakers. Indeed, in some immigrant groups these marriage brokers continue to work, arranging marriages for clients, sometimes in different countries. Most Western dating agencies take on clients by getting them to fill in a questionnaire with biographical details and preferences. These are then matched to other clients, and the agency gives them the opportunity to meet each other. Unfortunately, whether the agencies work by computer or by ordinary manual matching techniques, the chances of meeting a perfect match by this means are quite small. It is probably better if you can find an agency with a large number of clients, since then there is a wider choice. You would still have to keep an open mind as to the chances of success, and it might be better to treat it as a kind of trial and error process to be entered into for the sake of experience.

Speed dating

The use of 'speed dating' puts a number of self-selected people in a kind of blind date situation, and they have three minutes to chat with each prospective partner to see if they would like to date them. The chances of getting together sexually are apparently quite high, but whether these relationships last is not known.

Singles' clubs and bars

These are very variable, and the better ones do provide a friendly and cheerful atmosphere where you can meet new people. There is, however, especially among the male clients in these clubs, an expectation that the women they meet will be ready for sex on the first date, and this may not be the best way to meet someone who is looking for a longer-term relationship. Misunderstandings can arise in this situation, when perhaps one partner is interested in a one-night stand while the other is more interested in forming a steady partnership.

Advertisements in newspapers and magazines

These are like the dating agencies but without any kind of checking procedure. The danger is that you may meet someone who has sexual needs that may not match yours, and may even turn out to be risky to you. There are some couples who have met in this way and get along very well, but in many other cases the outcome has been either embarrassing or even traumatic for one of the partners.

The internet and dating apps

The internet has a great variety of dating and sexual chat rooms, and most of the time these are harmless. One of the most established online local classified advertisements site with forums for personal meeting opportunities is craigslist. 'A second chance at love for singles over forty' is the offer made by 'just senior singles'. However, even here you may find people posing as something they are not, so, as with all these routes to meet another person, you should be careful who you get in touch with, especially if it then leads to a face-to-face meeting. We suggest you should always meet for the first time in a public, reasonably busy place, preferably during the day.

More recently there has been a growth in the number of 'apps' that are downloadable onto smartphones and that can quickly identify other individuals in close vicinity who are also looking for a casual hook-up or to start a relationship on a 'no-strings basis' (no strings attached – nsa). Most of these apps offer immediate registration and upload of your profile. Be careful with what you mention on publicly viewable sites and think carefully when asked if you would like to upload a photograph. The apps provide an opportunity to view and read other profiles and often give ready access to other individuals (or couples or groups) looking to establish some kind of relationship or sexual experience.

Some of the more established apps will allow real time discussion with others, and although registration and basic use of the facilities of the app are often free, be aware that some require payment before actual contact can be made and this may mean sharing credit card details.

One of the largest companies that 'empowers users around the world to create new connections that otherwise might never have been possible' is Tinder, who claim over ten billion matches in nearly two hundred countries. The largest demographic age group is twenty-five to thirty-four years of age (45 per cent). Other dating apps include zoosk and elite.

Monogamous relationships or an affair?

Dating apps also provide the opportunity for individuals to meet other married or partnered people. One site that is often mentioned in the media is Ashley Madison who claim to have around fifty million members worldwide 'looking for a discreet connection' by using their internet site and app. A recent study found that around one in five people report having consensual non-monogamy (CNM) at some point of their lifetime. Many other people will have an affair without the knowledge of their partner. If they are found out, then as we mentioned in Chapter 10, this may be grounds for divorce or separation, although sometimes both partners will want to try to understand what has caused this to happen and to find a way to repair their relationship using some of the techniques we have mentioned throughout this book. People who identify as gay, lesbian or bisexual are more likely than those who are heterosexual to declare engagement in CNM. Thirty per cent of users of Tinder admit to being married.

The recent development of specialist apps has also allowed men who have sex with men (MSM) – or those who would like to meet with other men – the opportunity to meet men in a discreet setting. As around one in ten men identify as gay or bisexual (see below), this opportunity has seen considerable registrations on apps such as Gaydar and Grindr. They allow married men, men in relationships and single men to meet with other men wanting sex that is often described in graphic detail. There are a number of risks that are similar to the other routes of meeting another individual; although some argue that as these sites are more clearly aimed to attract other men wanting sex, the risks of unsafe sex or exploitation are more than marginal. For men who prefer some kink to their relationship as we mentioned in Chapter 7, the Recon app and website has helped some people go on to meet their partner.

One note of caution we should mention is the use of alcohol and other substances that you may think about before meeting someone through any of the routes above. These may disinhibit you and reduce anxiety as we mentioned earlier, but they may also make you take more risks and do something you subsequently regret. One study has shown that as people get older they are less likely to have safe sex, by not using a condom on their first date. Specifically, for gay or bisexual men who use drugs to facilitate and meet other men, the so called use of 'chemsex' is of particular concern. Risky sex to try to improve your confidence or get rid of the negative feelings of low self-esteem and loneliness is likely to lead to significant regret, and we will share alternative strategies that will hopefully be helpful to you.

What if you are afraid of close relationships or shy, socially unskilled?

Overcoming shyness

Shyness is one of the difficulties that may stand in the way of your forming a relationship. Shy people are often unusually sensitive to what others may think of them. They go around almost expecting that people will have a low opinion of them and not want to know them. This can of course develop into a vicious circle, with the shy person avoiding contact with others and never challenging that belief by finding out that some people actually like them. If you can overcome the habit of keeping to yourself at gatherings, at work or on holidays, you may find that it is not so difficult to get together with like-minded people. It is probable that some of the people you are afraid of are just as shy as you are, and you may be able to help them to be more outgoing themselves. There is no shame anyway in admitting that you are shy or self-conscious, and a potential partner may be attracted by that side of your personality. Try to think positively, in spite of your inner doubts and fears. Have faith in your own likeability. Think back on other situations, perhaps in school, in which you were approached by others wanting to make friends with you, and then try to go into the present situation with happy memories. Make your main focus of attention the other person you are with, what they are saying and how they seem to be feeling in themselves, and try not to think about whether they like you or not. Getting involved in a joint activity, such as a cause or voluntary work, can help you to make friends, and then the problems with finding something to talk about can be made a lot easier. There are many useful ideas and techniques to be found in the companion book in this series, Gillian Butler's *Overcoming Social Anxiety*.

Dealing with low self-esteem

This too is quite a common problem affecting single people who want to get into relationships, and it may go together with fear of intimacy (see below). If you feel that you have little to offer a partner, it may be very difficult for you to approach anyone with confidence. A reasonable level of confidence is in itself a good basis for forming relationships, and if you can begin to believe in yourself a little more you will have a better chance of beginning a relationship. There is a whole series of treatment approaches to help those with low self-esteem, and these include challenging your preconceived ideas and predictions, fighting your tendency to criticise yourself and enhancing self-acceptance. The companion book in this series, Melanie Fennell's *Overcoming Low Self-Esteem*, offers a guide to helping yourself to overcome your own low self-esteem, using the above techniques among many others.

Getting comfortable with emotional intimacy

This is another problem which can inhibit those who would like to be in a relationship. There are many types of intimacy, as we explained in Chapter 2, and one of these is emotional intimacy. Some people, particularly young men, have a fear of opening up their emotions to friends or potential partners, and they need to develop ways to overcome this. For example, if you have this problem you might experiment with being more open in small areas of your life, areas which are not very near to your inner feelings, such as your enthusiasm for something such as cars. Experience in this area can help you to open up more at parties or in places where you might be able to meet partners. It will gradually become easier as you practise it, and then you will be able to be more open and confident in talking about a wider range of subjects. Another way to help yourself in this respect is to think more positively, believe in yourself and give yourself positive feedback when things go well for you.

Associated with this problem is the issue of shame. This can be about your body, your previous sexual history, your sexual orientation or sexual preferences. If these exercises do not bring about the change you hope for, there may be a need to seek some specific help from a psychotherapist and you should discuss this with your GP or healthcare professional.

Social skills and how to improve them

Your problem of not being able to get into relationships may be due to your lack of social skills. This is not always associated with shyness, or with low self-esteem, but it can be a bar to making meaningful relationships with people, whether for sex or friendship. The first thing to remember in a social situation is that it helps to smile. This encourages the other person, and if you make eye contact at the same time they will feel more positive about you. Don't sit too far away or too near, as both can have the effect of putting the other person off. Try to keep your tone of voice quite relaxed, and don't come across as too intense. Try to keep up a flow of conversation, which contains a mixture of general topics, talk about you and talk about the other person. The most common thing that people with social skills problems complain of is that they can't think of what to talk about. It might be a good idea to think up a few useful topics in advance, to use when the conversation dries up, and you can feed them in when the time is right. Recent items of news, especially those that are entertaining, would help: also discussion of television programmes or recent sporting events. If the other person asks a question, try to make your answer more than just a yes or no, but more of a new idea with the possibility of further discussion. It is not, however, a good idea to keep the conversation going too long, especially in the early stages after meeting someone new. If you like them, make an arrangement to meet them again, and keep them interested in the things that you haven't said as well as those that you have.

CASE EXAMPLE

Gemma, a single woman in her late thirties, was seeking help with her difficulty in forming relationships. She didn't smile very much in the session, and the therapist asked her to try a social experiment on herself. She should try smiling whenever she was with other people, and see what the results were. In the next week she smiled a lot, and she was asked out on two dates, one of which led to a long-term relationship.

How much do you really want sex?

Some men and many more women have a sexual drive which is not biologically compelling. They can go for long periods without sex, and may not feel that the lack of it is a major problem for them. If you are like this, there is probably no urgent need for you to get into a sexual relationship, and you should then consider the possibility of a platonic, companionable relationship with someone. If you are comfortable in the person's company and have some shared interests, you should probably cultivate their friendship, and you then have the option of going for a more intimate relationship with them in due course, or keeping the friendship as it is. In fact, it is generally found that people who move from friendship to sexual interaction on the way to marriage usually have a more stable relationship than those who get attracted sexually and try to develop their friendship later as a couple. This suggests that it is often better to meet potential partners through mutual interests rather than because of sexual attraction (see above), and there is no problem with moving towards a more intimate relationship by this route. It should not be a reason to feel different or left out, but problems may arise either if your chosen partner has a very high sex drive compared to yours, or if you both have a low sex drive and want to have a family (see Chapter 7 for more advice on this situation).

Sexual orientation

If you have difficulty in forming heterosexual relationships, it may be because you are looking for someone who, for you, is the wrong kind of partner. You may have to consider your sexual orientation. As we mentioned above in the section on dating apps, there are a number of ways you can go about exploring your sexuality before deciding what you are most comfortable with. There is also much more information available now on the internet and from healthcare professionals. Although there remains some hostility and stigma about homosexuality, many people establish and have stable, life-long same-sex relationships. There is now an equal age of consent for sex of sixteen across the UK. Same-sex marriage has been possible in England, Wales and Scotland since 2014 following on from earlier legislation on civil partnerships introduced in 2005.

The most revealing question to ask yourself is 'Are my sexual fantasies centred on partners of my own sex or the opposite sex?' This also applies to watching passionate or explicit scenes on television or in films: are you more interested in the person of the same sex or the opposite sex? If your attraction is largely or exclusively towards your own sex, it would be sensible to think about talking to someone you know who is gay and deliberating about the possibility of 'coming out'. The answer to these questions might, however, depend on your age at the time: if you are very young, you might leave it for a few years before you make the decision, because sexual orientation is not necessarily fixed in teenagers, and your preferences may alter. In any case, many people are bisexual, and attracted more or less equally to both sexes. If you are still young, or if you are clearly bisexual, you might leave the decision as to whether to 'come out' until you meet someone of either sex with whom you feel comfortable. Whatever your orientation, the general advice in this chapter should be helpful, since the process of dating, entering a relationship and making it permanent is similar whatever your orientation.

A survey in 2015 reported that between 64 per cent and 80 per cent of gay men from black, Asian and minority ethnic (BAME) backgrounds accessing a gay website had encountered racism and they had been blocked on apps or called racist names. Nearly two thirds of the black and south-east Asian men interviewed said that racism on the gay scene was a bigger issue for them than homosexuality. Many of these men are objectified by white men and there remains an imbalance in many of the relationships that are established (just as there are in heterosexual relationships across race and culture). If there is any possibility that racism may exist or that this may have happened in a previous sexual encounter, try to communicate and share this experience, however painful, early in any new relationship to ensure any possible prejudices are recognised and dealt with early on in the relationship.

Gender identity

Transgender people are trans men, trans women and other people whose gender identity or gender expression differs from their assigned sex at birth, typically as a binary male or female. It is separate and different from sexual orientations so the trans male or trans female can be straight, lesbian, gay, bisexual, or asexual.

An increasing number of people choose to live their lives openly as a non-binary person with increasing visibility in the media and a striving by advocacy groups for official recognition. As people become more aware of the issues of gender dysphoria, the individual may come to recognise that the sense of gender identity that they have experienced, perhaps since the age of seven, is only now possible to describe, partly because the words to be used are relatively new and also because there have been very few visible role models in the media and politics until recently. This recognition can have a considerable impact on a relationship and the family. Increasingly, society is more accepting of diversity of gender than it is of sexual orientation and the stigma associated with both is decreasing but not yet absent. If these issues arise in your relationship, try to access professional support as soon as possible, in the knowledge that for many couples the opportunities to negotiate and continue together are much more common than existed just a couple of decades ago.

Moving from meeting to having a sexual relationship

Take it fairly slowly at first

Generally this is something you should be careful about. On the first date it is probably better to get to know each other, perhaps doing a little flirting and exploratory touching, but not getting into a deep sexual relationship there and then. Again, you have to remember that romantic and sexual encounters are shown in films and on television because of their dramatic impact rather than showing life as it is. Don't expect to fall into each other's arms on the first meeting, but take it more slowly, and get to know each other first. It's also usually unrewarding to have a sexual encounter just because you want the experience, or just to please the person you are with, if you don't feel attracted. This doesn't mean, however, that you have to be 'in love' with each other in order to get together sexually. The sexual interaction may happen for all sorts of good reasons, only some of which are to do with love. But a good deal of unhappiness can come from entering a sexual relationship for the wrong reasons.

Have you thought through the next moves after sex happens?

If you are attracted, it is better to allow sex to grow out of your general relationship. It is also sensible to think through some of the complications that may follow if you are going to go on meeting and if you are going to 'become an item' as the relationship deepens and you get closer. Have you considered what might happen if one of you stops desiring the other, or you decide not to go ahead with becoming a couple? There are many 'one-night stands' in which one of the two partners is disappointed that it never went further, and they did not go on to have a long-term relationship.

Fear of physical intimacy

Some people find it difficult to touch and be touched. This can be a limitation when it comes to entering a new relationship, because so much of the exchange in this phase is to do with physical touch. A casual touch on the hand or shoulder can be a good start, and this can then lead on to more intimate contact if it seems right, for instance if you are dancing together. One possible approach if you are very fearful of touch is to go to a situation such as dancing lessons, in which you are expected to touch your partner as part of the process. Another way to tackle this fear is to go for a massage, at a fitness centre or similar place (we mean just for a body massage, not for the more intimate services which are sometimes offered), and allow the masseur or masseuse to help you to get used to being touched. The main therapeutic change is likely to happen when you feel so used to being touched that it isn't an issue for you anymore.

Fear of sexual intimacy

The fear may be of sexual intimacy, which may be overcome by some of the exercises suggested in Chapter 7, as long as the partner is prepared to cooperate. If, however, you are without a partner, and can't even get close to having one because of your fears, you may need to use a cognitive approach on yourself to get 'psyched up' for the sexual encounter. You could give yourself cognitive self-statements about being a success if you have achieved a little more than the last time you attempted it. The key is to take it little by little, without scaring yourself or your potential partner by your attempts. We mentioned earlier that some people have a concern about the shape or size of their genitalia: it is usually more the fear of being seen in the nude than of having sex with someone. We suggest that you ensure that you are relaxed (including breathing deeply and slowly) before starting with any intimate conversation or touching. Take some time to repeat some positive statements about yourself including that you love yourself for who you are and that you love the person you want to be close with for who they are. Neither of you should try to prejudge or change anything about each other at this stage, but rather try to approach each new encounter with joy and curiosity about the other person. Try to appreciate that in the vast majority of relationships, people are attracted to each other for who they are and their personality rather than solely for their physical attractiveness and rarely for the size or shape of their genitalia or breasts.

What if one of you has a sexual dysfunction or sexual problem?

These are not at all uncommon, as mentioned in Chapter 3. Sometimes one of the partners is older, and in this case the sexual response may not be as rapid and enthusiastic as the other one expects. Be prepared for this, especially if you are an older man and your new partner is younger than yourself. Similar problems may arise if you have had sexual problems in the past, and this can apply to either men or women in the new relationship. Whatever the problem, it should be hinted at quite early on that there may be some difficulty the first time that sex happens (see Chapter 7 for further help with this situation).

Do you bring other responsibilities into the new relationship?

If you are entering the new relationship having broken up with a previous partner, you may be looking after your children, either as the main carer or at weekends and on holidays. We think that it is important to make this clear to the new partner early in the relationship, and not to spring it on them as a surprise during a visit. There are other complications that can arise, for example if you are still seeing the previous partner and feel that you do not want to be disloyal by rejecting them too quickly. It is better to slow down the progress of your new relationship until the previous one is clearly over.

Declaring that you are in a serious relationship

This is sometimes more difficult than you expect, not only because you have to tell your relatives (including any children) about the new situation (see Chapter 11), but it may be that previous partners are still 'on the scene' and may feel sufficiently rejected by your entering into a new relationship to make difficulties for you as a couple. Again, it helps to discuss this well ahead of the possible crisis, and work out a strategy as a couple for dealing with it. You have to be fairly confident in the stability of the new relationship to declare to others that it is a reality.

If the new relationship is a same-sex one, the process of declaring it to friends and family can be complicated by the need to 'come out' as well. This may lead to problems with parents (see below) and with friends and acquaintances. Although there is general acceptance of gay and lesbian relationships in Western society there is still a fair amount of conscious and unconscious prejudice that may need to be dealt with.

Introducing the new partner to your parents

In new relationships the question usually arises as to whether and when to introduce your partner to your parents and other family members. You have to remember that your relationship with your parents goes back as long as you can remember, while the new relationship with your partner is very young. This means that the new relationship is more fragile than you probably thought, and crises can occur if you don't plan the meeting carefully. For example, it might be better on the first visit to have an exit strategy from the meeting if things get too difficult, and you should also share with your partner what your parents are like and how you relate to them. Discussing the visit afterwards can illuminate your own insight into your family, but you should be careful not to become too defensive if you feel that your partner is critical of them. You are then faced with a 'triangle' as described in Chapters 4 and 6, and you will have to employ your skills as a negotiator in helping your partner to fit in with your family and vice versa.

Explaining to other friends and acquaintances

Similar problems may occur in letting others know that you are now an 'item', and there may be some conflicts of loyalty, especially with those friends with whom you have had an emotionally intimate confiding relationship. As advised in Chapter 6, the new couple should act as far as possible as a team in this situation, as long as they are both committed to their future together, and this may mean becoming more distant from old friends and indeed old partners.

Is the new relationship good enough to commit yourselves to living together?

Sometimes the crises brought on by these introductions and readjustments are sufficiently serious to lead to the partners doubting whether the new relationship is viable. If you feel this way, it may be better to reconsider your future together before making the decision to move in together. It is harder to break up after this has happened, and it becomes more of a trauma at that stage. However, if you are both clear that living together is the right thing to do, you should then go ahead with the planning.

Your place or mine (or somewhere different)?

If you still feel confident enough to move in together, then you should do so. It will often be that one of you will move in with the other, rather than getting a new place as a couple. There can be territorial difficulties here, in that the person whose place it is may have feelings of ownership of the space, and be less than fully tolerant of the new partner and their ways (see the case example below). This is something that should be negotiated (see Chapter 5) and you should be sensitive to the other person's needs over these issues. The main difficulty is with putting both of your belongings in the space that one of you previously occupied alone. Then there are problems such as whether you have separate places for your things or not. These questions may seem trivial to the couple who move in together to share their lives in a glow of mutual passion, but in reality they usually come up at some time or other, and it is better to be prepared for the difficulties than to stumble over them when you have been living together for some months. The process of moving in is a good test of your mutual abilities to negotiate and communicate (see Chapter 5), because it is all a question of being positive towards each other and giving as well as taking. It needs to be taken as seriously as any major life decision.

CASE EXAMPLE

Maurice (57) and Vivienne (56) had been married for two years; both had been widowed. She had three daughters and he had two, all the girls being in their twenties. They had moved into the house where Vivienne had lived with her husband, and there were a number of territorial tensions. For example, her daughters had the run of the house, while Maurice's girls had to ask Vivienne's permission before visiting. Maurice always felt that he was in her house rather than theirs. Vivienne was emotionally volatile and outspoken; he was quiet and diplomatic. The problem was that, although his sex drive was fairly high, he was diffident about approaching her, partly because she might be critical if things did not go well. Eventually their territorial dispute was solved when they agreed that the daughters should all be treated more or less equally, and he asserted himself over some other domestic arrangements. Their sex life improved as his confidence grew.

A half-way stage

If you have great difficulties in solving the problems of sharing space (and this can be worse for those who have lived alone for a long time before moving in together) then it might be sensible in the early stages to keep your separate places, and to stay together only some nights of the week. This way you will gradually acclimatise to being together full-time, and you can then decide at leisure if and when the time is ripe to move in full-time.

Choosing a place jointly

This is often a safer option than moving in to one partner's place, because the territorial issues are not as acute if neither of you has put their mark down before the other moved in. On the other hand, moving is a traumatic event in itself and if both of you are moving, the trauma is potentially doubled. However, you will avoid the territorial issues that we mentioned above. In the long run this is the best option, because one partner's previous residence will always be seen as being preferentially theirs.

Joint or separate activities – to share or not to share

This remains an issue for many couples long into their relationship. They may have got together mainly through sexual attraction, and may not have many shared interests. Some couples accept this, and work on the basis that they don't do many things together except at home. Others prefer to try to share their lives more, and this can be easier if they got together out of mutual interests and friendship rather than purely through sexual attraction. The most important aspect of the problem is for the couple to work out a reasonably comfortable way of living together while both carrying on a satisfying life, either together or separately, outside the home.

Shall we get married?

This is more a matter of choice than it was several decades

ago, when most couples who lived together were in fact married. Now there are many different arrangements, of which marriage, civil partnerships and cohabitation are just three options. Marriage is still quite an undertaking, not only because of the legal aspects but because of the social statement that you are making and the fact that it implies more of a lifelong commitment than simply living together does. However, there are obligations, rights and responsibilities in sharing your home with another person if you do not marry. The impact of the death of the owner of the property on inheritance and the welfare of any children (should there be any from another relationship) is not always straightforward and it is worth clarifying the current situation with a solicitor who can advise you, taking into consideration your actual circumstances.

Marriage as a potential stress to the relationship

In some couples the relationship has continued quite comfortably while they are living together and enjoying social and leisure activities, until they decide to get married. Then an increased level of conflict may lead to intractable difficulties between them. In some cases it is to do with the marriage increasing the expectations on both sides that they will do more together, that each will be more compliant towards the other and that life will be easier. This usually doesn't happen, and the process may set up a tension between expectations and reality which both find disappointing. The fact of having more security as a couple, and feeling that the commitment on both sides is greater, may compensate to some extent for these tensions, and make the couple more stable, but all couples who marry after living together for a time should be wary of the stresses that go with settling down as a married couple. In reality they both have to work harder than before, and need to use negotiating and communicating skills more than they have had to when previously living together.

How about having children?

Some couples of course have their children before they get married, but for many of them the fact of marrying is a catalyst for wanting children, and the two contribute fairly equally to their sense of stability and togetherness. Either way, the decision to have children is a big one, and while for some couples having children is easy, for others it is a major problem, with infertility and in vitro fertilisation needed, especially if they start the process later in life. Some prefer to leave having children until they have their own house, but for others it is a decision that is made for them by unprotected intercourse and the passions of the moment. In this day of having what one wants very easily in other areas of life, it can be quite frustrating to some couples that it is difficult to conceive children, and for many couples the restriction of their lifestyle following the birth of children is a major stress. Prospective parents should consider these issues before committing themselves to parenthood.

The family life-cycle

Observant readers will have noticed that, in developing the topic of how to get into relationships, we have come full circle, and have entered the area that we explored in Chapter 1. The family life-cycle, as presented there in its rather simple and well-ordered form, begins with the couple meeting, then forming a relationship, getting engaged, getting married and having their first child. In a way, the whole book has been somewhat circular in this way, and of course we are dealing with a series of repeating circles in talking about relationships which spiral down from one generation to the next, complicated by increasing changes in society and our secular lifestyles. We hope that the book has given you some insight into the problems inherent in relationships and the solutions that can be found through goodwill, hard work and ingenuity. The long-term stability of families may be enhanced if couples can find better ways to communicate and to negotiate so as to remain together and provide the much needed support that helps children to grow up and form satisfactory relationships of their own.

- You may be quite content to be single, so don't let social or media pressures force you to enter relationships.
- The best way to get to know potential partners is through everyday contacts at work, classes, sports activities, etc.

- Ideas are presented as to how to use dating agencies, singles' clubs, magazine advertisements and the internet.
- Suggestions are given on how to overcome shyness and low self-esteem.
- Ideas on improving comfort in social situations and improving social skills are offered.
- You should be clear whether you really want a sexual relationship, and also what your own orientation is.
- The stages of moving from friendship through sex to living together, then having children and marrying, are outlined.

In conclusion

What should be your take-home message as readers of this book?

We could begin with the fact that it is more difficult to sustain a relationship now than fifty years ago (see Chapter 1). But, having said that, we think that it is still a worthwhile thing to attempt, for several reasons:

- A good relationship with a partner has a positive influence in maintaining your health.
- Divorce and separation are traumas in the same league as bereavement.
- Divorce is expensive.
- Second marriages or similar relationships with children are usually complicated.
- A stable relationship between two parents is still probably the best setting in which to bring up children.

In almost every marriage or long-term relationship the thought occurs at one time or another as to whether the partners should continue together or separate. The message that we would like to get across is that it is better to think about how to improve the relationship rather than planning to end it. The expectation is that the relationship will become so much more rewarding when you communicate and negotiate better that you will want it to continue.

The various problems that affect relationships are explored in Chapters 2 and 3, with special emphasis on the theories underlying this work, the difficulties that men and women have in communication with each other, and the ways in which people's individual styles and personalities may bring them into conflict. This doesn't mean that relationships involving 'opposites' are doomed, but the partners in this kind of relationship may need to be more than usually tolerant of each other to make it work.

Although it is true that not all relationships can be saved, there are many which could be greatly improved with goodwill and the techniques that we have been describing in the chapters from Part Two onward. The more important of these are:

- How to tackle relationship problems (Chapter 4)
- Timed discussions (to avoid conflict, see Chapter 5)

- Negotiating rather than complaining (Chapter 5)
- Better communication (Chapter 5)
- Being a good behaviourally orientated therapist and rewarding your partner for what you want from them (Chapter 5)
- Using timetables for areas of conflict (Chapter 6)
- Learning to argue and resolve arguments (Chapter 6)
- Developing greater empathy (Chapter 6)
- Sorting out the boundaries of the relationship, whether these involve children, family, friends, hobbies, sports, activities or work (Chapter 6)

Most of the above ways of tackling problems will be easier to apply if you are able to cooperate on them and work together as a couple. However, in Chapter 5 we have also given you some hints as to how to improve your relationship when working unilaterally. This is not as easy as when you are working together, but there is still a good chance that you will be able to make a significant alteration in your partner's behaviour without the partner actually being involved in the plan.

There are some other, more specific, areas which you might need to work on, such as:

- Communication about the sexual side (Chapter 3)
- Solving sexual problems (Chapter 7)
- Coping with illnesses (Chapter 8)
- Domestic abuse and violence (Chapter 9)

These areas are very important in the stability of a relationship, and if they are badly handled they may spell the end of an otherwise good partnership. But if they are dealt with well, problems in these areas can actually make the relationship more rewarding. All this may, however, be in vain, and one must be realistic enough to acknowledge that not all marriages or long-term relationships can be saved. If it really doesn't work for you, you may think about the question of separation and divorce. In that case it may help to look at Chapter 10 and the section on having a 'good' divorce. Then the question of a blended family may arise, and Chapter 11 may provide you with some ideas about how to do this more successfully while avoiding some of the pitfalls.

Lastly, if you are not currently in a relationship, the suggestions in Chapter 12 may be of use in helping you to overcome some of the difficulties you face in trying to begin a relationship. We also consider issues should you choose to have any kind of extramarital (or non-monogamous) relationship.

The central message of the book, which should be reiterated here, is that you should never despair of the possibility of change in your relationship. The point is made at several stages in the book that if you change your own behaviour you will probably see a corresponding change in your partner. Ultimately, of course, the only person you can really change is yourself, but a different approach to the relationship on your side will very probably bear fruit in the form of a change in your partner's behaviour.

If you are working together as a couple, one of the most helpful things to remember is that it is more important to stabilise the relationship than to get your own way or to win an argument. In the last analysis the systemic approach teaches us that it is really nobody's fault when things go wrong, but just the accumulation of repetitive sequences between the two of you that leads to a kind of vicious circle. The key is to find a way of breaking that circle and finding another way of interacting.

It would be sensible to remind you here that the methods we have been advocating are not expected to 'cure' a relationship problem, such that you can then rest and let things happen in the old way. The methods are essentially ones which you must continue using, and it helps to remember that, even if things go very well for a time as a result of good communication and negotiation, it would be worth your while to return to the issues from time to time in order to refresh your techniques.

The 'can do' attitude that we have been trying to pass on is one that will take you far, even on a 'do-it-yourself' basis. However, if it all becomes too much and you find that you can't solve your problems without outside help, there are some very good therapy and counselling services available, which we have given details of in Useful addresses.

We do hope that the advice given in this book will help you to ensure that your marriage or long-term relationship is satisfying, fun, stable, intimate and enduring.

Useful addresses and contact points

Organisations providing therapy, counselling or information

British Association for Behavioural and Cognitive
Psychotherapies (BABCP)
Imperial House
Hornby Street
Bury
BL9 5BN
Tel: 0161 705 4304
Fax: 0161 705 4306
Web: www.babcp.org.uk
email: babcp@babcp.com

British Association for Counselling and Psychotherapy
BACP House
15 St John's Business Park
Lutterworth, LE17 4HB
Tel: 01455 883300
Fax: 01455 550243
Web: www.bacp.co.uk

College of Sexual and Relationship Therapists (COSRT)
PO Box 13686
London, SW20 9ZH
Tel/fax: 020 8543 2707
Web: www.cosrt.org.uk
email: info@cosrt.org.uk

Institute of Family Therapy
24–32 Stephenson Way
London, NW1 2HX
Tel: 020 7391 9150
Web: www.ift.org.uk

Relate (The Relationship People)
Premier House
Carolina Court
Lakeside
Doncaster
DN4 5RA
Tel: 0300 100 1234
Web: www.relate.org.uk
email: enquiries@relate.org.uk

Tavistock Relationships
70 Warren Street
London, W1T 5PB
Tel: 020 7380 1975
Web: www.tccr.org.uk

United Kingdom Council for Psychotherapy (UKCP)
2nd Floor, Edward House
2 Wakley Street
London
EC1V 7LT
Tel: 020 7014 9955
Web: www.ukcp.org.uk

International organisations

Association for Behavioral and Cognitive Therapies
(ABCT, formerly AABT) USA
Tel: (00 1) 212 647 1890
Web: www.abct.org

National Institute of Mental Health (NIMH)
Tel: (00 1) 301 443 4513
Web: www.nimh.nih.gov
email: nimhinfo@nih.gov

Relationships Australia
Canberra
Tel: 02 6162 9300
Web: http://www.relationships.org.au
email: media@relationships.org.au

AAMFT
American Association for Marriage and Family Therapy
112 South Alfred Street
Alexandria
VA 22314-3061
USA
Tel: (00 1) 703 838 9808
Web: www.aamft.org

The American Psychiatric Association
1000 Wilson Boulevard
Suite 1825
Arlington
VA 22209-3901
USA
Tel: (00 1) 703 907 7300
Web: www.psych.org
email: apa@psych.org

The Canadian Psychiatric Association
141 Laurier Avenue West
Suite 701
Ottawa
Ontario
K1P 5J3
Canada
Tel: (00) 613 234 2815
Web: www.cpa-apc.org
email: cpa@cpa-apc.org

Organisations providing general information about related areas

British Psychological Society
St Andrews House
48 Princess Road East
Leicester, LE1 7DR
Tel: 0116 254 9568
Web: www.bps.org.uk
email: enquiries@bps.org.uk

Royal College of General Practitioners
30 Euston Square
London, NW1 2FB
Tel: 020 3188 7400
Web: www.rcgp.org.uk

Royal College of Psychiatrists
21 Prescot Street
London, E1 8BB
Tel: 020 7235 2351
Web: www.rcpsych.ac.uk

Organisations involved in substance abuse and its management

Alcoholics Anonymous UK
Tel: (helpline) 0800 9177650
Web: www.alcoholics-anonymous.org.uk

Alanon
Tel: 020 7403 0888
Web: www.al-anonuk.org.uk

Narcotics Anonymous
Tel: (helpline) 0300 9991212
Web: www.ukna.org

National Association of Children of Alcoholics
Tel: (helpline) 0800 358 3456
Web: www.nacoa.org.uk

International organisations

AA World Services, Inc. (USA)
Tel: (00 1) 212 870 3400
Web: www.aa.org

Al-Anon Family Group Headquarters Inc. (USA)
Tel: (00 1) 757 563 1600
Web: www.al-anon.org
email: wso@al-anon.org

Al-Anon Family Group Headquarters (Canada) Inc.
Tel: (00) 613 723 8484
Web: www.al-anon.org
email: wso@al-anon.org

National Association for Children of Alcoholics (USA)
Tel: (00 1) 301 468 0985
Web: www.nacoa.org
email: nacoa@nacoa.org

Organisations that may help with domestic violence

In an emergency always ring 999

British Association of Anger Management
Tel: 0345 1300 286
Web: angermanage.co.uk

Men's Advice Line (domestic violence)
Tel: 0808 801 0327
Web: www.mensadviceline.org.uk

National Centre for Domestic Violence
Tel: 0800 9702 070
Web:www.ncdv.org.uk

Refuge National Domestic Violence Helpline
Tel: 0808 2000 247
Web: www.refuge.org.uk

Victim Support Service
Tel: 0808 1689 111
Web: www.victimsupport.org.uk

Women's Aid National Domestic Violence Helpline
Tel: 0800 2000 247
Web: www.womensaid.org.uk
email: info@womensaid.org.uk

Organisations that may help with psychiatric illness

BiPolar UK
11 Belgrave Road
London
SW1V 1RB
Tel. 0333 323 3880
Web: www.bipolaruk.org
email: info@bipolaruk.org

MIND (The National Association for Mental Health)
Granta House
15–19 Broadway
London
E15 4BQ
Tel: 020 8519 2122
Web: www.mind.org.uk
email: contact@mind.org.uk

Royal College of Psychiatrists (see above)

Providers of sexual health information

Fpa (Family Planning Association)
23–28 Penn Street
London
N1 5DL
Web: www.fpa.org.uk

Sexual Advice Association (SAA)
c/o Right Angle 224
Building 3
Chiswick Park
566 Chiswick High Road
London
W4 5YA
Tel: 0207 486 7262
Web: http://sexualadviceassociation.co.uk
email: info@sexualadviceassociation.co.uk

Providers of sexual aids

Owen Mumford Ltd
Brook Hill
Woodstock
Oxfordshire
OX20 1TU
Tel: 01993 812021
Web: www.owenmumford.com

Further reading

Ansari, A. & Klineberg, E., *Modern Romance*, Paperback: London: Penguin 2016; Consideration of the romantic options available through dating apps, mobile phones and social media.

Crowe, Michael & Ridley, Jane, *Therapy with Couples* (2nd Edition), Oxford: Blackwell Scientific Publications, 2000; A book for therapists using the techniques that we have described here.

Fisher, H., *Why him? Why her?*, New York: Holt 2010; Recognising the complex nature of romance and attachment gives insights into the essence of dating, finding lasting love and marriage.

Hall, P., *How to have a healthy divorce,* Chatham: Vermilion 2008; Using the experience as a chance for personal growth and development allowing a future with realistic optimism.

Hertlein, K., Weeks, G. & Gambescia N. (Eds), *Systemic Sex Therapy* (2nd Edition), Hove: Routledge 2015; A book for therapists using many of the techniques that we have described here.

Levine, S. B., *Barriers to loving. A Clinician's Perspective,* Hove: Routledge, 2014; Considers the many factors that affect partner lovability, feeling and expressing love and aspirations to love and be loved

Wylie, K. (Ed.), *ABC of Sexual Health,* Chichester: Wiley

Blackwell, BMJ Books 2015; An overview of sexual and relationship issues for clinicians.

Self-help books

Beck, Aaron, *Love is Never Enough*, New York: Harper and Row, 1988; A self-help book for relationships using Beck's own Cognitive Behaviour Therapy approach.

Butler, Gillian, *Overcoming Social Anxiety and Shyness*, London: Constable & Robinson, 2016; A book in this series with much helpful advice on social skills and social confidence.

Fennell, Melanie, *Overcoming Low Self-Esteem*, London: Constable & Robinson, 2016; A good guide to improving self-esteem.

Gilbert, Paul, *Overcoming Depression* (third edition), London: Constable & Robinson, 2009; One of the most successful and popular books in this series.

Gray, John, *Men are from Mars, Women are from Venus*, London: HarperCollins, 1992; A readable and light-hearted but also serious book about the miscommunications that occur between men and women.

Metz, M. E. & McCarthy, B. W., *Enduring Desire – Your guide to life long intimacy,* Hove: Routledge, 2010; A book that considers the problems occurring over the lifetime of a relationship.

Schnarch, D., *Resurrecting Sex: Solving Sexual Problems and Revolutionizing Your Relationship*, New York: Quill, 2003; A good read for couples to help resolve their sexual problems using compassion, generosity and integrity within the relationship.

Yaffe, Maurice & Fenwick, Elizabeth, *Sexual Happiness: A Practical Guide*, London: Dorling Kindersley, 1986; Still probably the best guide to dealing with problems of sexual desire and function.

Index